Negotiating
NAFTA

THE WASHINGTON PAPERS

. . . intended to meet the need for an authoritative, yet prompt, public appraisal of the major developments in world affairs.

President, CSIS: David M. Abshire

Series Editor: Walter Laqueur

Director of Studies: Erik R. Peterson

Director of Publications: James R. Dunton

Managing Editor: Donna R. Spitler

Editorial Assistants: Kathleen M. McTigue, Shannon Cantrell

MANUSCRIPT SUBMISSION

The Washington Papers and Praeger Publishers welcome inquiries concerning manuscript submissions. Please include with your inquiry a curriculum vitae, synopsis, table of contents, and estimated manuscript length. Manuscript length must fall between 30,000 and 45,000 words. All submissions will be peer reviewed. Submissions to *The Washington Papers* should be sent to *The Washington Papers*; The Center for Strategic and International Studies; 1800 K Street NW; Suite 400; Washington, DC 20006. Book proposals should be sent to Praeger Publishers; 88 Post Road West; P.O. Box 5007; Westport, CT 06881-5007.

The Washington Papers/173

Negotiating NAFTA

A Mexican Envoy's Account

Hermann von Bertrab

Foreword by
Sidney Weintraub

**PUBLISHED WITH
THE CENTER FOR STRATEGIC
AND INTERNATIONAL STUDIES**

 PRAEGER

**Westport, Connecticut
London**

Library of Congress Cataloging-in-Publication Data

Bertrab, Hermann von.
    Negotiating NAFTA : a Mexican envoy's account / Hermann von
Bertrab : foreword by Sidney Weintraub.
      p.   cm. – (The Washington papers : 173)
    "Published with The Center for Strategic and International
Studies".
    Includes index.
    ISBN 0-275-95934-1 (cloth). – ISBN 0-275-95935-X (pbk.)
    1. Free trade – North America. 2. Free trade – Mexico. 3. Free
trade – United States. 4. Mexico – Commercial policy. 5. North
American Free Trade Agreement – History. I. Title. II. Series.
HF1746.B469 1997
382′.917 – DC21   97-39527

The Washington Papers are written under the auspices of the Center for Strategic and International Studies (CSIS) and published with CSIS by Praeger Publishers. CSIS, as a public policy research institution, does not take specific policy positions. Accordingly, all views, positions, and conclusions expressed in the volumes of this series should be understood to be solely those of the authors.

British Library Cataloguing in Publication data is available.   *HF1746*

Copyright © 1997 by The Center for Strategic and   *.B469*
International Studies   *1997*

Library of Congress Catalog Card Number: 97-39527
ISBN: 0-275-95934-1 (cloth)
      0-275-95935-X (paper)

First published in 1997

Praeger Publishers, 88 Post Road West, Westport, CT 06881
An imprint of Greenwood Publishing Group, Inc.

Printed in the United States of America

The paper used in this book complies with the Permanent Paper Standard issued by the National Information Standards Organization (Z39.48-1984).

10 9 8 7 6 5 4 3 2 1

Contents

Foreword

O wad some Power the giftie gie us
To see oursels as ithers see us!
It wad frae monie a blunder free us,
*   An foolish notion:*
What airs in dress an' gait wad lea'e us,
*   An' ev'n devotion!*
    Robert Burns, "To a Louse," 1786

The discussion that led to the creation of the North American Free Trade Area was—arguably—the most important negotiation between the United States and Mexico since the Treaty of Guadalupe Hidalgo of 1848. The treaty, following the Mexican war, led to U.S. annexation of half of Mexico's territory and left a tradition of hostility in Mexico toward the United States that has not disappeared in almost 150 years. Although that was not its central purpose, NAFTA was the most comprehensive effort since then to eradicate this legacy.

NAFTA represented almost everything Guadalupe Hidalgo was not. The latter resulted from a conquering U.S. army's imposing its will on a weak Mexico; NAFTA was a negotiation based on formal equality of two sovereign nations. The negotiations to conclude Guadalupe Hidalgo were difficult, but based on how much one side would win and the other would lose; the objective of NAFTA, in the shorthand language used for these purposes, was to create a win-win situation. With modest modifications in the period between the two negotiations, relations between Mexico and the United States were cool; the two countries, in the language of Alan Riding's popular book, were "Distant Neighbors." The two countries are much less distant as a result of NAFTA.

Hermann von Bertrab's book is not an analysis of whether NAFTA is good or bad for either country. The assumption for concluding the agreement was that the linking of the two economies in the ways that NAFTA accomplishes would be good for each. This is the implicit starting point for von Bertrab's discussion. We will see in due course, in ten years or even more, whether the basis on which NAFTA was created was correct.

There will be adjustments on each side. Shocks will rock support for the economic integration, as we saw following the economic collapse in Mexico in 1995. The ultimate test, however, is not whether there will be hard periods in the relationship, or trade and other conflicts, but rather whether these are resolved more expeditiously than would have been possible without the agreement. Will total trade increase more with than without NAFTA? Will NAFTA create habits of cooperation that did not exist before, and will these be institutionalized in ways that were impossible before? If, over time, NAFTA is not win-win, it will not endure.

The negotiations did not resolve all issues. NAFTA thus spawned scores of meetings among officials of the three member countries—Canada, Mexico, and the United States—and between their private sectors. NAFTA will be deepened as the three countries reach understandings on industrial, communications, transportation, environmental, labor workplace, sanitary, phytosanitary, and other standards. Case histories will be created as disputes arise and are settled. Legal structures will be altered to deal with novel situations. There are still persons in both countries who appeal to nationalism and the absolutes of sovereignty to destroy NAFTA, but the larger picture is that border demarcations have diminished for economic relations in North America, as they are diminishing globally.

Von Bertrab does not deal with these larger issues, but the reader should keep them in mind in order to put in perspective the extent of emotional insularity of NAFTA naysayers. What von Bertrab does provide are insights into the complexities of the negotiation, the interests that had to be mollified in each of the countries, the compromises that were required to reach the final text. These insights come not from a U.S. perspective, or from a neutral one, but from a Mexican deeply engaged in the details of the day-to-day negotiations. U.S. readers do not often get this outside view of their own political personalities and negotiators from a knowledgeable insider on the other side of the bargaining table. They usually hear from their home-grown partisans, just as the Mexicans hear from their own. (Von Bertrab's book has been published in Spanish, and the Mexican edition follows the normal practice of hearing from one's own.)

Von Bertrab is well equipped to provide this perspective. He was recruited from the Mexican private sector to coordinate the Washington office of the Mexican negotiating team. The Mexican cabinet agency in charge of the negotiations was the Secretariat of Trade and Industrial Development (SECOFI in its Spanish initials). Von Bertrab had previous exposure to the United States, from the time spent to earn a Ph.D. in economics at The University of Texas at Austin. (I can relate to this milieu because I taught at UT/Austin for some 20 years and am now Dean Rusk Professor Emeritus in its Lyndon B. Johnson School of Public Affairs.)

The NAFTA negotiations were difficult not only because they addressed bread-and-butter issues for businesses and consumers in the three countries, but because the negotiators had to overcome many fundamental conceptual differences. With regard to the U.S.-Mexico aspect—omitting the Canadian participation for the moment—the two countries have vastly disparate levels of economic development, and this asymmetry caused problems for each on the speed of tariff and nontariff reduction and on how labor in the two economies would fare as these border barriers disappeared. The negotiators had thoroughly different cultural formations, although many of the Mexicans, like von Bertrab himself, attended U.S. universities. U.S. negotiators, by contrast, generally had little prior exposure to Mexico. The distancing of the two countries brought on by their separate histories had to be narrowed. Stereotypes, often quite mistaken, had to be overcome. Particular interests had to be satisfied – labor, environmentalists, small producers, multinational corporations, generators of intellectual property, farmers, and many more.

This volume provides insights that a U.S. reader would not normally consider. The Mexican negotiators had to learn how U.S. society makes economic decisions. Most Americans are not sure of this themselves. But it was particularly difficult for the Mexican negotiators to learn how to take into account the local interests of 435 U.S. representatives and 100 U.S. senators in their negotiating positions. The book contains many fascinating anecdotes on the workings of business and the U.S. Congress, between the Congress and the executive branch, and on the operations of the many nongovernmental organizations in the United States. Mexico has its own lobbying groups, but they are less numerous and quite primitive compared with the complexity of those in the United States. How these single-issue groups function is well nigh impenetrable for foreigners to fathom, which explains why Mexico, like other foreign governments, find it necessary to hire U.S. lobbyists. A comprehensive trade negotiation is a bonanza for law firms, other lobbyists, and public relations groups, and the discussion in this book makes clear why this is so.

There are brief but fascinating discussions of many of the key personalities who were involved in the NAFTA process, directly and indirectly, on the U.S. side. These include Congressman Bill Richardson of New Mexico, a supporter of NAFTA; Pat Choate, who voiced the views of Ross Perot in opposing the agreement; Carla Hills, the U.S. trade representative, to whom von Bertrab refers as the "crystal lady" (a takeoff on Margaret Thatcher as the "iron lady") because of her combination of charm and substantive knowledge; Julius Katz, the deputy U.S. trade representative, who is characterized as tough but honest; and Congressman Richard Gephardt, who voted for the fast-track legislation that permitted the negotiations to proceed, but then opposed most of the trade liberalization that resulted.

For those interested in national negotiating styles, von Bertrab notes that decision-making in Mexico is concentrated at the top, whereas the process is more decentralized in the United States. U.S. negotiators, he says, tend to start by seeking agreement on general principles, whereas the Mexicans look almost immediately for tradeoffs. The difficulties caused by the different legal structures are brought out.

The overall negotiation was complex, but nowhere more than in working out the rules of origin (that is, how to determine how much North American content was necessary for a product to qualify for free trade) for textiles, textile products, and autos. One of the strengths of the book is that it presents the nature of specific sectoral negotiations as seen from the Mexican side.

Von Bertrab describes us—the United States when engaged in a comprehensive negotiation—in ways we do not describe ourselves. We are at once self-centered and expansive, rigid and flexible, and overbearing and prepared to compromise. The overall picture is neither good nor bad, but sui generis. The strength of this book is that it provides the insights of an informed and observant outsider to help us see ourselves as others—to be precise, one other—see us.

Sidney Weintraub
Center for Strategic and International Studies
Washington, D.C.

September 1997

Introduction

NAFTA is a rediscovery of common interests among three countries that have often parted ways over the years. In a single historical act, Columbus discovered the New World and started the modern age. The discovery brought an encounter of cultures: of the West with its Graeco-Roman and Christian roots and of America the continent where the Mayas, the Incas, and the Aztecs flourished. This clash unleashed an enormous energy that had already started working in the Renaissance and truly created a New World.

All American countries are bound together from their origins. They share the common legacy of European societies that encountered Native Americans in ways not always the pride of humanity. The three founders of NAFTA in particular share intertwining historical paths. In colonial times Mexico was "New Spain"; one of the most important segments of what would become the United States was "New England"; the original section of present Canada was "New France." Although each country went its own way, each's development cannot be understood without the presence of the other two. Mexico is integral to the history of the southwestern United States, and Spanish explorers put Florida and the Chesapeake Bay on the map. The first U.S. dollar bills, which were issued by authority of the Continental Congress, were backed by the Spanish (that is, Mexican) silver peso. The United States and Canada are historically linked in the exploration and settlement of the North American continent's whole central region from the Great Lakes to the Gulf of Mexico, and in many other ways—from the influence of the legitimist families to the lives of such great people as Thomas Edison.

Although the origins of the three countries cannot be separated, the three are divided by their traditions, prejudices, and interests. Mexico is much more heavily "native" American than the United States, which is oriented more toward Europe. The history of Mexican-U.S. relations has been troubled—for example, the war of Texas, the U.S.-Mexican war, the U.S. Marines' landing in Veracruz. This history was embodied in Mexican president Lerdo de Tejada's nineteenth-century statement: "Between them and us, the desert!" Ever since, the United States and Mexico have lived as "distant neighbors," developing "back to back" while ignoring, or trying to ignore, each other. Yet all along there have been flashes of recognition and understanding. At the beginning of the 1760s, when the Spanish regulations that forbade trade with countries other than Spain were abolished, the port of Veracruz received more vessels from the northern British colonies—and later from the United States—than from Spain. The ideals of the American struggle for independence has inspired generations of Mexican politicians.

NAFTA has been a process of rediscovery in other ways as well. For Mexico it means rediscovering and accepting the United States as a partner and friend; for the United States it means rediscovering the broader concept of America and relating to American neighbors less harshly and inimically; for Canada it means rediscovering the presence and importance of countries to the south with whom it has had but tenuous links.

This process needs time to mature and cannot in a single stroke resolve the varied, complicated problems arising from conflicts between the countries. Indeed the broadening of trade and other economic relations will only increase the causes for conflict. But the new framework defined by NAFTA is better suited to address new, and old, problems than the ancient one of mistrust and will make it easier to analyze and correct controversies as they arise—even those beyond the scope of NAFTA.

The process of joint exploration that brought NAFTA into

being has made NAFTA much more than a trade agreement. NAFTA's strong, unique personality not only is shaping the future of the signatory countries, but is setting global precedents. NAFTA represents the first time a trade agreement has

- involved negotiations between highly developed countries and a third world country and between two neighboring countries that have been divided by huge cultural differences and historic rivalries.
- incorporated the revolutionary process of modernizing a backward country, blending for the first time the idea of development (in contrast with the many theories important in past agreements) with the idea of free trade.
- included the United States, emerging from "splendid isolation," in a role as less than the unchallenged, predestined center of the economic universe. The parties to NAFTA have accepted the new challenge of adapting to global economic competition.
- given Mexico the opportunity to lead the hemisphere in defining and accepting a new relationship with the United States and Canada. In NAFTA, Mexico accepts the existence of a neighboring country it had always viewed with suspicion and fear and plans to build its future upon such acceptance.
- achieved mutual respect and understanding between two political systems with substantially different operating styles and establishes certain conditions of transparency that contribute to further transforming the Mexican political system.
- initiated and successfully implemented accommodations between the environment and trade. As the greenest of trade agreements, it sets a pattern to be debated and followed in the future.
- addressed labor conditions among totally different countries and establishes a system to resolve serious disagreements that may arise. This is of particular importance because some have regarded the whole concept of the agreement as based upon differences in wages and labor conditions. Further, such considerations drew emotional reactions, and the groups with tremendous political clout that represent, at least officially, labor's interests were aggressively and directly involved.

• involved negotiations with two different U.S. administrations and thus became part of the electoral debate that preceded the change in administrations.

Differences in underlying principles and motives have also complicated the process. The agreement Mexico wanted—one that would primarily entice flows of investment capital into the country—was portrayed in a recession-bound United States as tantamount to the giving away of jobs. The United States considered the agreement in geopolitical terms, which offended Mexican feelings. In terms of investment, the highest U.S. priority was the energy sector, the area in which Mexico adamantly guarded its traditions and was least willing to make concessions.

This volume recounts the clashing of visions and interests and the struggles to surmount prejudice and misunderstanding that finally shaped NAFTA into a pathbreaking instrument whose world-wide impact will reach far into the twenty-first century. Even the political, social, and economic developments in Mexico since 1994 cannot be adequately understood without understanding the momentum and hurdles created by NAFTA and the links between the United States and Mexico that it has strengthened, beyond the letter of the agreement itself.

My participation as chief Mexican representative for NAFTA in the United States gave me a unique, first-hand perspective on the inner workings of the U.S. political system and insight into its meaning for Mexico. Given my vantage point, I refer only occasionally to Canada, its relevance notwithstanding. My work is primarily a memoir—a story told as it was lived and perceived. Although my account is not intended to be exhaustive and scholarly, care has been taken to check the facts. It is, as Huck Finn would have said, "mostly true." Sufficient analysis is included to examine and integrate the parts to assess NAFTA's overall meaning.

Like four acts in a play, this narrative proceeds in four stages—the fast track, the negotiations, the political stage and side agreements, and ratification. Each act includes a certain tension, dramatic episodes, and a temporary outcome that sets the stage for the next act. The unique personality and peculiar tensions of each act produced an end result unforeseen by those whose courage, creativity, and honesty initiated the process.

At different stages, the U.S. representatives either joined forces or sat at opposite sides of the table with the Mexican representatives. This itself provided a special drama. During the fast-track and ratification stages, the overall interests and aims of the U.S. and Mexican administrations merged. Even there, however, ideas differed about the game-plan and how to implement it. The political interactions between Congress and the administration, combined with the roles played by the various interest groups at work within them and the fluctuations of public opinion in both countries, made it very difficult—in the context of domestic confrontation—to define Mexico's role as an ally of the United States.

The aim of the whole process—the development of free trade—may seem coldly theoretical. But such an objective does not become real without the crisscrossing of different interests, the drama of colliding cultures, and the passions of the people intervening in it. The process involved more than an elegant idea brought to reality through NAFTA. It was a warm, conflictual, deeply human story—and the subject of this volume.

Negotiating
NAFTA

1

The Fast Track

Under the "fast-track" process, the U.S. Congress can authorize the president to negotiate specified trade agreements. A special ruling stipulates that any agreement reached must be presented to Congress for an up-or-down vote, forestalling amendments. This procedure, which grew out of a perceived need to negotiate with other countries in good faith, allows approval of an agreed-upon text without the almost continuous renegotiation of the usual amendment process. Foreign countries would otherwise hesitate even to begin the process of negotiations.

U.S. academicians and politicians–Sidney Weintraub, Bill Richardson, and Lalo Valdez–had previously proposed a free trade agreement between the United States and Mexico, and apparently U.S. president Ronald Reagan himself had discussed the issue. But it was not until Mexican president Carlos Salinas, reversing his prior refusal to consider such an agreement, proposed the concept to the U.S. government that the wheels were set in motion. Decisions are not made when they are announced, and in this case the turning point occurred in 1990, on a January evening in Davos, Switzerland.

There, in Davos, a Mexican delegation led by President Salinas was attending a meeting sponsored by the World Economic Forum, during which delegation members were becoming acutely aware of the new global realities that were changing the framework of international relations. At the time the Europeans were totally engrossed with the problems and expectations arising from the crumbling walls of communist Europe. Europe was confronting its own problems, and a distant country like Mexico (even if engaged in a strenuous effort to modernize its economy and society) was of little interest to European policymakers at this particular time. One night, after a long day of discussing the issue, the delegation members went to their rooms. Exhausted, Secretary of Commerce Jaime Serra-Puche lay down and began to doze without noticing that his door was ajar. He was awakened later by the sound of the door opening. To his amazement, the president walked in and, standing in front of him in his nightgown, asked: "Jaime, what do you think about asking the United States to enter into a Free Trade Agreement?"

Serra could not go back to sleep. The next day he met U.S. Trade Representative Carla Hills in a lobby and approached her about the issue. Mrs. Hills's eyes opened wide in disbelief, and she answered: "Well, Jaime, we ought to talk about that with President Bush." Thus began the process.

A period of consultations ensued in each country, and the decision was made to begin the formal phase negotiations. It was a momentous decision for Mexico, whose foreign policy had been defensive and its economic policy isolationist. After an exchange of letters among the presidents, the U.S. president requested authorization from Congress to engage in negotiations. And thus began the "fast-track" process.

The Mexican government then decided on a plan and an organization to face the challenge. In October 1990, Herminio Blanco, undersecretary for foreign trade, was named chief negotiator for the agreement. He contacted me, whom he had known for many years, and asked me to accept a not yet fully defined position in Washington, D.C., as head of a Mexican government office that would guide the process of negotiation toward the final ratification of an agreement.

Dr. Blanco had been my student at Mexico's Monterrey Institute of Technology, and since then we had been close friends. As a student, he was nonchalantly brilliant–an easygoing, tall kid from northern Mexico who was the son of a small general store owner in the mountains of Chihuahua. He later on went on to earn a Ph.D. in economics from the University of Chicago. It never occurred to me that he would consider me for this project. At the time I was busy running my own small, but adequately successful, business—Imerval, a securities training institute with a fairly good reputation in the Mexican financial industry. Nevertheless, Blanco sought me out for the job, and one Friday in October told me he had the president's approval and would I please take the job.

Later I reflected on what could have motivated his request, aside from our mutual trust and my familiarity with the United States. I possessed some experience in starting new businesses, and this agreement would be a totally new venture. Also, I would be returning to my business when the mission was over. Given that the path ahead would be full of political landmines, a person not pursuing a political or public service career could act and offer advice more freely and effectively. In addition, I would be given great latitude to put together a task force consisting of a Mexican staff members and U.S. consultants. The task force would totally focus on establishing a free trade agreement. The issues between the two countries were manifold and complex, and consideration of them had to be separate from the central one involved. We would have to define the issues and our goals clearly and develop strategies for firmly pursuing them.

Understanding U.S. commercial laws was comparable to exploring the labyrinth of Knossos. We would have to navigate a maze of laws and institutions—the Omnibus Law of 1988, Special 301, Super 301, Commerce Law of 1974, the International Trade Commission, the Office of the United States Trade Representative, the Advisory Committee on Trade (ACTPN), a roster of advisory commissions (IPAC, APAC, LAC, DPAC, SPAC), etc.—and face their convoluted relations with the diverse committees of jurisdiction in the legislative branch.

Although this process was enormously complicated, we had to grasp the underlying concepts that provided a certain coherence. Everything had to be understood within the framework of relations (1) between the administration and the legislative branches, with Congress granting rights to the executive but at the same time vying to control the process; (2) between the openness of the largest market in the world and its persistent trade deficit, which created great contradictory pressures (pressures that became apparent in 1974 with legislation that simultaneously established the fast-track mechanism, thereby facilitating commercial agreements and widening the availability of countervailing duties and anti-dumping regulations—an arsenal of weapons frequently used to force on other countries the protectionist interests of some U.S. corporations); and (3) between the sectors that were protectionistic by tradition or need and the ones seeking to open foreign markets in a context of globalization that imposed necessary, but at times unwelcome, transformations. Thus, diverse forces were at work that, like ocean cross-currents, made proceeding hazardous. Certainly we had undertaken, at our own substantial risk, the goal of achieving a free trade agreement with the United States. Another extremely important variable in the equation was the ongoing process of the Uruguay Round within the GATT agreement. Our initial bilateral proposal—multilateral after Canada entered the process—had to compete for political and legislative attention with the Round.

The fast-track process allows for an expeditious consideration of trade agreements, but is in fact a quite convoluted affair. Before Congress can grant negotiating authority to the president, it must first receive an official request from a foreign government, allowing Congress to determine whether the proposed objectives are consonant with the objectives of U.S. trade law. In the Mexican case, a letter from President Carlos Salinas, signed on August 21, 1990, proposed to President Bush the negotiation of a free trade agreement. In turn, President Bush notified Congress in letters to the House Ways and Means Committee chairman Dan Rostenkowski and the Senate Finance Committee chairman Lloyd Bentsen that he intended to enter into such negotiations. He informed them also that Canada wished to participate. Acting through both committees, the Congress then had 60 legislative days (days when Congress is in session) to consider the request and vote affirmatively or let the deadline pass without a vote, thereby yielding authority to the president.

Depending upon the number of legislative session-days, this

step would probably take until late February or early March 1991. Although this exercise was necessary to ensure the will to negotiate and in principle could have allowed the negotiations to start, its meaning was mostly symbolic. The president's fast-track authority, within which these negotiations would be integrated, would expire in June 1991 (the legislation had been passed for a two-year period in May 1989). The president would have to request an extension of his fast-track authority three months before expiration in March 1991. Even aside from the Mexican trade agreement, an extension of the fast-track authority would be necessary to proceed with the GATT negotiations that had stalled in Geneva in December 1990, owing to the many differences that had arisen, especially between the United States and the European Community. Two legislative hurdles thus had to be surmounted: the chance of disapproval of the Mexican negotiations and the extension of the fast-track authority.

I was surprised to hear from our lawyers the first of several "good faith" inconsistencies in the U.S. system. A sword of Damocles would be hanging over the whole process even after Congress had authorized the president to proceed. For example, if members of Congress did not believe that the executive had consulted fully with them, a reverse fast-track procedure could start that would nullify the initial legislative decision. We were persuaded that this entailed an important but theoretical statement of Congress's prerogatives, which to me exceeded the bounds of logic in a legal sense and anyway seemed quite unnecessary, given that Congress could always vote down any proposed agreement. Yet it powerfully recognized the opinion Congress has of its rights, as was probably the whole intention. We had to understand the logic behind certain aspects in congressional procedures that were impervious to our Cartesian thinking and prepare for unforeseeable legislative events that to us seemed to bend reality. At least twice early on, during the second and fourth congresses, the House held two legislative days in one calendar day! We were assured that the recurrence of similar decisions was extremely unlikely. I was baffled at this prerogative, which nevertheless clarified the overpowering capabilities of the Congress and its commanding presence in U.S. society.

Putting the Team Together

In Mexico a structure was established with young, competent, and creative civil servants who set about defining the issues with the active support of private groups organized as the Coordinadora de Organizaciones Empresariales de Comercio Exterior (COECE). COECE comprised the six most important sectors of the economy—from manufacturing industries to agriculture and insurance services. The actual day-to-day work was done in sectoral work-groups that started preparing papers analyzing the different sectors' positions from the start of the process. These would make their most important contribution later during the negotiations proper. Nevertheless, even at this early phase they were extremely cooperative and encouraging. The chairman of COECE Juan Gallardo was an intelligent, indefatigable partner in our endeavors. Highly personable and articulate, with a profound grasp of both the Mexican and U.S. systems and cultures and a good understanding of business and politics, he provided invaluable insight and help. His deputy Guillermo Güemez, an experienced and optimistic former banker, was with his cordial manner and grasp of the issues a most welcome participant in our enlarged team.

In the United States, the Mexican team was being organized and integrated into the Mexican embassy, although it would carry on a special mission in a separate venue nearby. I had the full support of Mexico City, and the usual bureaucratic entanglements were disposed of. We only vaguely understood how we should organize and assign different tasks. The idea evolved of a platoon working tightly together with a common purpose but undertaking flexible assignments as conditions required. Borrowing from Chinese philosophy, I insisted that we should work the way water works. Water is the most forceful of natural elements because all its molecules—its drops, as the Chinese would put it—are simple and close together. This togetherness does not entail the rigid structure of a rock, which is breakable. You cannot "break" water because its molecules are tightly but flexibly bound. Water's power comes from its invariable gravitational push or sense of direction. And so should we be: uncomplicated people, working flexibly together in unwavering single-mindedness toward a common mission.

·I did not choose my team for their specific professional experience, whether in trade, economics, or politics. I chose them for such basic human attributes and skills as intelligence, ability to work hard, and team spirit. They should have some degree of experience in the United States. Most of them were young, which gave us a special energy and drive. From the International Monetary Fund, I got Ildefonso Guajardo, an economist from Monterrey with graduate studies in Pennsylvania. I was able to get two people from the World Bank—Harvard graduate Eduardo Wallentin and Luis de la Calle, who had a Ph.D. in economics from the University of Virginia. José Angel Canela had been teaching at Carnegie-Mellon University in Pittsburgh and had an unusual and extremely valuable academic background, with studies both in Mexico and the United States, as a lawyer, a sociologist, and a statistician. Felix Aguilar, who had performed his graduate studies at the University of Boston, was the only member who joined the team from the Mexican civil service at the Ministry of Commerce. José Treviño and Rodolfo Balmaceda came with me from Mexico. José had studied foreign relations in Mexico and later been involved in the financial sector at a brokerage firm. Rodolfo, an economist from the Monterrey Institute of Technology who had worked for me two years previously, was employed by a Mexican investment bank.

The members of this initial team proved to be excellent choices. Everyone left a promising career for what was to be a stupendous adventure. The concept of the trade agreement was a powerful draw. Rodolfo Balmaceda was just about to get married when I asked him to join the team. With courage and youthful spirit he gave up a good-paying job and immediately after his honeymoon, with the obvious and necessary support of his wife Ana Luisa, joined us in Washington.

The Opponents

While the team was taking shape, the battle was already raging: our opponents had captured the stage, and their armies were at work in Congress influencing public opinion. The proponents were unprepared and disorganized. The opposition was motivated by group interests but also by various principles, and people driven by principles fight much more fanatically than those simply defending a particular set of interests.

The "fast track" was merely a procedure to facilitate a free trade agreement. Arguments against the fast track were really against the concept of a free trade agreement with Mexico. Some members of Congress were unwilling to grant the administration a right that is constitutionally theirs. But this was not the opponents' real concern. Thomas Donahue, a high-level official in the AFL-CIO with whom I later had some polite conversations that simply glossed over the issues, warned that the use of the fast track would "dilute the law-making authority of the Congress"— a disingenuous argument that disguised interests behind a cloak of high-minded verbiage.

Opposition to the idea of free trade has a fascinating social and political history. Traditionally the Democrats had been free-traders and the Republicans protectionists, but their roles had changed. Now a Republican president who held the strong support of most of his party was pushing for free trade. Traditionally, Democratic administrations had been much more receptive to Latin American issues and had led Franklin Roosevelt's "Good Neighbor" policy and John F. Kennedy's "Alliance for Progress." The roles were now reversed. Our former friends had become our opponents.

But our problem was not to understand the fluctuating historical trends in the United States. Profound changes were moving Mexico away from its traditional protectionism and fear of foreign involvement toward trade and friendlier relations with the United States. And thus the virulent, almost inimical attitude of many U.S. groups confused us. We thought we had a good cause that would benefit both countries and were reaching out, only to find ourselves in political turmoil.

The opponents were most afraid that free competition with Mexican workers would lower U.S. wages. At this stage, however, the two governments had decided not to consider worker migration, which would have given much more force to their argument. But fears persisted. People were not persuaded by the counterargument that average U.S. wages would instead rise, given that the export of more highly skilled goods would transfer people from lower wage to higher wage sectors. As Massachusetts lost its low-wage textile industry, it acquired higher technology manufacturing. But fears can be blind to comforting counterarguments, and the trade unions were one in their fierce opposition.

Other more abstract, but solid, arguments did not sway them either. A free trade region would raise the welfare of the countries involved because the rationalization of production, larger markets, and increased jobs would make them more efficient. Fear and partisan political interest made them impervious to such reasoning. A cartoon published at the time spelled out the problem with wit and clarity. A sailor on the high mast of a man-of-war spies a small canoe with a little Mexican happily rowing along in his sombrero, and the sailor cries out "Pirates!" For a comparatively small, poor country, it was almost a distinction to be that feared by the world's mightiest superpower. Although we smiled occasionally at that, we had to take the fear seriously.

People fight harder to prevent losses – real or imagined – than to achieve gains. NAFTA gave so many people such a general fear of loss that they were not ready to contemplate a win-win proposition. At this early stage before a negotiated agreement, specific sectors had little reason to feel threatened. But the specter of low-skilled jobs in labor-intensive industries persisted throughout the whole process. To better understand the political effect that such fears could have, we researched the positions that several noted trade unions were taking on the issue. We found all of them opposed. Many of them had became members of the "Coalition for Justice in the Maquiladoras," a protectionist institution masquerading as fighting for justice for the Mexican worker. We had very little sympathy for the trade unions' concerns, as we understood them, and I personally had to control my outrage at their sanctimonious claims and gross exaggerations. An officer of the Communications Workers of America said, for example, that Mexico threatened to "pull the rug out from under the livelihoods of thousands of American workers" – actually a modest statement if compared with later ones that raised the figure to millions! Similar positions were taken by unions that realistically had more to gain than to lose–the United Paperworkers International Union and others whose activities were totally unrelated, such as the American Federation of State, County, and Municipal Employees. Much of this could be certainly explained as fraternal support. But other political considerations may have been behind this position as well–numbers and power. Organized labor represented more than 30 percent of the labor force in 1960. Its decline to 15 percent in the 1990s has led to internal divisions. We knew about tensions between Lane Kirkland, president of the AFL-CIO, and Thomas Donahue.[1] Given their internal dissensions related to their search for a new meaning in the modern world, we understood NAFTA was not of great concern to them. But politically NAFTA provided a convenient way to rally the faithful to an old-fashioned defense of workers' jobs and wages against an intruding foreign country,

The job issue had its pros and cons, but we were taken aback by the malicious arguments of the environmentalists. Mexico had recently approved environmental legislation that was certainly not in all respects adequate, and enforcement was lax. As a country, Mexico was in the first stages of developing an awareness of environmental problems and faced many other claims on its limited resources. No one could argue that it was at the level of the industrialized countries' standards. But all this had nothing to do with NAFTA. If anything, NAFTA would improve Mexico's ability to deal with environmental issues. Why people should oppose NAFTA for environmental reasons was always a great perplexity. Opponents argued that polluting industries would locate in Mexico to rid themselves of clean-up costs, thereby acquiring an "illegitimate" comparative advantage and increasing the world's problems. But the real issue at the time was simply the concept of a trade agreement. In my opinion, the consistent position would have been to insist during the negotiations on conditions that would help clean up the environment without opposing the concept of the agreement itself before it had any content. Some people eventually saw it this way, and in due time environmental groups would join our side.

There were two explanations for that attitude: disguised protectionism and mistrust of the Mexicans' sincerity in their efforts to clean up. Some proclaimed their fears that spurring industrialization would aggravate Mexico's pollution problems—an argument that was either disingenuous or falsely paternalistic. All these made us angry—and sad. It was quite discomforting to have people rehash old prejudices without appreciating Mexico's decision to do something about its environment. The environmentalists of California or Colorado seemed more concerned about Mexico City's smog problems than the inhabitants of Mexico City itself. Preposterous. We knew there was a deep concern in Mexico about it and that efforts were being made to improve conditions; we also knew but that it would take a long time and require many resources also needed for other aims.

During that period in March 1991, the government shut down a $500 million refinery in Mexico City and halted operations at many other plants—at one point 140 of them. I personally felt a mixture of disgust and disappointment and actually told critics several times: "Come help us and cease throwing stones. A poor Mexico is a polluted Mexico. A richer Mexico will have the means to clean up its environment and provide healthier conditions. We have the will; we lack the necessary means."

Because I knew many critics were idealists, I believed that we ultimately would be able to win the support of many of them as well as unmask those who were using environmental arguments for strictly protectionist purposes. The *Los Angeles Times* had it right in its editorial of April 29, 1991:

> It would be disingenuous to argue that environmental issues are of no concern to free trade talks. But to insist they be part of the talks is also at best disingenuous and, at worst, downright cynical. Environmental issues can be dauntingly complex. Putting them on the table during trade talks is a sure way to slow the talks down and maybe even sabotage them.

We were initially rather naive regarding certain points of formulating and executing U.S. trade law and policy. Even the Commerce Law of 1974 had considered the possibility that a large increase of imports would significantly affect production and employment in specific industries. One of the law's remedies in those cases was to provide training for people laid off in the process. U.S. trade policy was in the process of reaching beyond strictly commercial issues—initially restricted to tariffs—to encompass not only nontariff barriers and intellectual property rights but even elements that were subsumed under the concept of a "Social Charter" that many NGOs thought should become a part of any trade agreement. The concept used in the European Community entailed a totally different type of economic and social integration, which fact did not hamper radicals from trying to impose similar tools to dissimilar conditions.

These concerns were publicized in such a way and with such a choice of language that they strongly affected Congress, which would have the final say on the matter and where would converge the activities of all the proponents and the opponents of a free trade agreement that could not be achieved without a fast track. Secretary of Commerce Mosbacher had said to a meeting of Texas businessmen: "If we don't have the fast track, your children will not be able to see the end of negotiations." That indicated in a nutshell the gist of the problem, and the determining factor was for Congress to give the agreement a chance.

Initial Contacts

In due course we would become acquainted with many members of Congress, some of whom became our staunch supporters. I was lucky to be introduced to Congressman Bill Richardson by Doda de Wolf, a distinguished Polish lady with whom my wife and I shared mutual Mexican friends. At a party at her house on New Year's eve, Bill immediately impressed me with his forceful and affable personality. We stood, drinks in hand, for the first of many conversations. I sensed from the start that he would put his considerable force—both physical and political—behind pursuing an intelligent strategy toward his objectives. And NAFTA became one of them. He obviously was inherently drawn to the idea because his mother is Mexican and also lives in Mexico, and his father was a noted U.S. banker with much experience and many friends there. As a representative from New Mexico, he was also disposed to improving relations with the neighboring country.

In early February 1991, I visited him, accompanied by Jaime Serra, Mexican secretary of commerce and the official responsible for the proposed trade agreement, and Herminio Blanco, chief Mexican negotiator, and experienced his tough tactics firsthand: He scared us. As things are currently going, he warned, we will lose a vote on a Mexican fast track. Dr. Serra, a strong and passionate man, emerged from the meeting anxious to revise our strategy even as we were walking down the steps of the Longworth building, the Capitol rising before us in the leafless, wintry park. I tried to smooth things by saying that Richardson's concerns were probably true under prevailing conditions but that conditions were certainly changing. Until then, the opponents had had a free ride in Congress, and the proponents, although slow in starting out, were beginning to organize. Nevertheless our efforts were energized, and Dr. Serra insisted on reviewing and reinforcing our action plan.

I was beginning to understand that members of Congress "keep their powder dry" until an issue comes close to decision. For each issue, nevertheless, a core of supporters has to be formed who will keep the issue continuously on their radar screens and determine the strategy to be followed.

We started focusing more intently on conveying information to members of Congress. We sent them fact sheets presenting Mexico's position on different issues, visited with them, and maintained closer contact with such private sector groupings as the Business Roundtable, which includes the most important – Fortune 500-type – U.S. firms, the Chambers of Commerce, and other trade associations representing varied business interests. We also initiated contacts with U.S. think tanks, where we found a great many capable, honest people. Most were inclined to favor free trade, even in more liberal institutions like the Brookings Institution. The Heritage Foundation proved extremely helpful, with Wesley Smith as an intelligent and enthusiastic supporter. The well-respected Center for Strategic and International Studies was a prime proponent of NAFTA, and three of its members—Sidney Weintraub, Georges Fauriol, and Delal Baer—co-signed a letter from leading academics in support of free trade with Mexico. We established contacts with, and received solid support from, the Hudson Institution, the American Enterprise Institute, and several other organizations. A strong majority supported the free trade agreement, but some, like the Economic Policy Institute, were adamantly opposed. One of its members Cale Marshall acted as an adviser to Rep. Richard Gephardt, with whom we would later experience problems, and its president Jeff Faux appeared in all the anti-NAFTA rosters. We learned, however, that because almost half of its funding originated in the unions, its opinions on the subject were biased.

Our activities would have been impossible without the help of highly qualified consultants. In time we would have a whole armada of them, including five government relations advisers and several law firms, with Shearman Sterling in the senior position. Burson-Marsteller, our public relations company, was the largest U.S. company of its kind and with its varied resources and experience made a creative addition to our team. Manchester Trade brought in very useful experience on commercial policy matters.

We could not put together our U.S. support team without facing the problem of lobbying as foreign agents in the U.S. political system. I had been acquainted with the discussion about Japan's purported outright influence-buying in the administration and Congress. An article by Pat Choate (who in my opinion would later lose all credibility by selling false arguments for the money of Ross Perot) presented Japan as "a foreign country running an ongoing political campaign as though it were a third major political party."[2]

I had my doubts about his credibility even then, but we took his analysis seriously and wanted to avoid any such criticism (although, as seen later, we would not be too successful at avoiding it). Anyway, a country like Mexico would not have to defend the type of special interests that Japan did and would be in no position to spend what the article—published by the reputable *Harvard Business Review*—estimated at $400 million a year. But we had to come to grips with the nature of lobbying by a foreign country and its potential for problems.

We received friendly advice from people at a think tank about the accepted role of lobbyists in the U.S. system. A constitutional tradition interprets the first amendment as affirming the right to petition the government for all people, even the ones unable to represent themselves effectively. Further, lobbyists promote critical information flow by providing new information to legislators above and beyond what they and their staffs would be able on their own to find and communicate about the effects of a given policy.

Be this as it may, we found the assistance of lobbyists extremely important. They helped us understand the intricacies of the U.S. legislative process where we were bound, willy-nilly, to be involved. There was no way we could have acquainted ourselves with the system without the intelligent help of our lobbying team. Mexican authorities were initially reluctant to retain people who might not understand Mexican concerns and would anyway be inclined to promote their own country's agenda. We discussed this issue and finally decided that because the agreement would in all honesty benefit both countries, there would be no problem as to split loyalties. I strongly insisted that they were to act professionally as any good accountant or lawyer would and decline to assist with anything that involved a conflict of interest. And I would be proven right. The professionalism of our lobbying team was beyond reproach. If lobbyists did not exist, we would have had to invent them, for we could not participate in a game without understanding its rules.

But there were also rules for the lobbyists themselves acting in behalf of foreign agents. We were extremely punctilious in abiding by all the regulations of the Foreign Agent Registration Act (FARA). Each one of our consultants was registered, even when they were not, in a strict legal sense, required to be—those, for example, who did not, as our advisers, deal in any way with authorities. Every one of them registered, and each quarter they provided a report about officials or members of Congress visited and the printed information that had been handed out.

We started visiting some of the members of Congress that could eventually become the whip group to carry on the task of getting the necessary votes for the fast track. My first impression of the corridors of Congress was both splendid and confusing. People came and went in groups or alone—it really was the people's house. The lobbies at the side of session halls were continuously busy with groups waiting on sofas for their representative to arrive or standing for a brief chat with a representative who had just come out of a session for a brief visit. The houses of Congress were democracy in operation: openness and transparency and a turmoil of activity—hearings starting under the watchful eye of TV cameras, people sitting in the small waiting rooms of representatives, or in the somewhat larger offices of senators. It was an exhilarating atmosphere, and I could feel myself absorbing some of the diffuse energy.

The members of Congress were a good representative sample of the colorful mosaic of the country, but for the most part one could see their similarities: highly articulate and personable, if not outright handsome, they possessed a strong sense of their role and importance. Given the multiple issues they are called to vote upon and the many requests of constituents they have to attend to, they have to rely on their own, or their committee's, staffers. I developed a great respect for many of them. Extremely well prepared and hard working, the staffers are advisers, research personnel, and errand runners all in one. They form the scaffold that gives structure to the whole and in their subtle way make the system work.

During my first few months in Washington, D.C., I asked for an appointment with the powerful chairman of the House Ways and Means Committee Dan Rostenkowski. We knew he could become a strong supporter and wanted to talk to him about the meaning of the agreement for Mexico and its benefits to the United States. As we sat down in the small conference room of his office at the committee, the chairman came in—a commanding personality and a strong, vigorous physical presence with large hands and a natural smile on his ample square face. After a few pleasantries, we gave him our message, which he followed with attention. In a loud, clear voice reflecting the weight of his personality, he replied that he had not made up his mind and had not heard from many of our friends, but had received visits from many of our opponents. He was the leader with clear political instincts, advising us what to do: go out and talk to your allies, trade associations, fellow Hispanics, and tell them to come and talk to me about it. I was greatly impressed by this engaging person, by the smiling, mischievous look in his eyes, and most of all by his shrewdness as one who sets the agenda and then pretends he is following.

It was a great lesson. We were encouraged by his attitude and learned that our role would have to be indirect, that it was the citizens and organizations of the country that had to put pressure on their representatives, and there lay our main task. When I had another opportunity to visit him, I asked whether he was hearing from our friends. He replied yes but mainly from the great bosses of the big companies who had come, as he put it, to "massage me with their cold hands." He wanted to hear from smaller companies, from plant managers, from associations closer to the political grass roots.

Later, the chairman had to relinquish his post because of the Post Office scandal, and his reelection bid was defeated. Whatever his involvement in those affairs, I greatly admired him as the quintessential ward politician who had emerged from tough Chicago politics with an engaging sense of humor, strong leadership skills, and rough honesty. [NOTE: Mr. Rostenkowski was later exonerated of some of the counts against him. One aspect of the politician's life that generates many problems was touched on in the opinion of Judge Ruth Bader Ginsburg in a federal appeals court ruling on the former congressman's case: "The life of a congressman . . . whose official day ends only after a round of nominally 'social' events at which he is obliged to appear . . . makes the line between 'official' and 'personal' services particularly difficult to draw."]

While our lobbyists explained to us the working of the system, the contact with members gave flesh and life to our understanding. Another important visit was to Senator Lloyd Bentsen, the highly respected and influential chairman of the Finance Committee. When we sat down in his office at our first meeting, he asked, with a gentle smile, "Now tell me, what ever happened to the land of mañana?" I answered, "It has become the land of today," and we spoke about the great strides Mexico was making toward modernization. He listened sympathetically and analyzed clearly and authoritatively the conditions for passage of the fast track in Congress. He was not that optimistic, but we knew he would act forcefully for it. On a later visit, just before the vote, he took from his shirt pocket a small piece of paper with the names of senators he was working on. There he was—the polished gentleman from South Texas, the son of a farmer with the distinguished elegance of an aristocrat. One could sense a strength of will and sharp intelligence beneath his warm, charming countenance. When he became secretary of the Treasury in the Clinton administration, we believed the cause of NAFTA had lost strong and wise support where it most counted—in Congress.

We visited with several other members of Congress at the time, but one of our most diligent, strenuous supporters and friends was Jim Kolbe, the Arizona congressman who on the Republican side became the whip that put together the necessary votes. I was always impressed by his shining optimism and intelligent energy. Staffers play an important role, and the first one I saw in action was Richard Kye, a Californian working at the time for Jim Kolbe. His energy, creativity, and optimism were infectious.

Although we certainly followed the wise advice of Chairman Rostenkowski, we continued calling on members of Congress with the purpose of creating good will. Given the shrill voices being sounded about Mexico, we thought one of our best strategies would be simply to give as many politicians as possible the opportunity to know us, to learn that Mexico was not an outlandish, exotic place, and to discover that we could be aware of their concerns and capable of articulating our positions in a manner they could understand. Our team, including visitors from Mexico, paid 325 visits to members of Congress during the fast-track process.

We visited also with the declared opposition. When I walked into Congressman Don J. Pease's office—at the time with Marcy

Kaptur, the leader of the agreement's opposition – I was impressed by the bust of President John Kennedy on his desk. We found common ground in talking about Kennedy because I had as a student been inspired by Kennedy's creativity. Pease was about to retire and, unbound by reelection strictures, seemed to understand our position and the merits of free trade. But he could not vote for it in opposition to his constituents in the heart of the rust-belt. I left with a good feeling and, although I thought he should probably show more leadership, was impressed at having met a man of integrity.

The clear definition of each member's position – or clear statement of the lack of one – struck me, a foreign observer, as manifesting the sometimes rugged transparency of U.S. society. It was surprising then to discover that hidden within the system were labyrinthine methods of skewing the system to make it less transparent and, yes, less democratic. One of my first eye-openers, so to speak, was the architectural set-up of the different spaces in the buildings, which intrigued me when I visited – for example, the Rules Committee room. I was aware of the committee's importance as the filter through which all House legislation has to pass. It decides which bills will be debated on the floor – and when and how. The committee's rather small room is dominated by a huge round table that looks disproportionate to the shape of the surrounding space. It is another way of saying, "Visitors are only selectively welcome." There the leadership finally acts and, some would say, manipulates the system. If that room serves as the door, certainly Representative Joe Moakley, a big imposing Irishman, looked very much like a no-nonsense door-keeper.

All congressmen and senators are equal to each other in various ways; they have their own local political base that makes those of them with safe seats strong political figures indeed. Otherwise the whole system is structured around a leadership structure that puts enormous power in the hands of the chairmen of the most important committees, with seniority as the determining principle. Financial contributors, among others, give disproportionate sums to sitting leaders and provide less leeway for a "circulation of the elites." In my opinion, the United States would be better served if some restrictions were imposed on the years one could chair a committee.

Campaign Strategy

With the helpful advice of many congressional members and our own consultants, we developed a multifaceted strategy: bringing high Mexican officials to visit Congress and give talks around the country; distributing information about Mexico; contacting friendly groups, particularly Hispanics; scheduling assorted speaking engagements; and finally setting up a "road-show" that included interviews on radio talk programs and editorial board meetings with the leading national and regional newspapers. My first and rather nervous Capitol Hill debut was at the competitiveness caucus, co-chaired by Ron Coleman (from El Paso) and Don Pease. If I did not do very well, nobody was rude enough to point it out. My first launching as a public speaker was at the Corn Growers Association Convention in Kansas City, a place replete with memories of Truman. With floodlights blinding my eyes, I was scarcely aware of the 1,000 people listening in the large hall. But the ready applause of those in the audience, and their countenance, once the houselights went on, gave me pleasure. In the next few years, I would serve as public speaker at similar—or smaller—events more than 360 times, and the rest of the team followed suit.

On February 5, 1991, Presidents Bush and Salinas and Prime Minister Mulroney announced their intention to pursue a North American Free Trade Agreement. Canada already had an operating Free Trade Agreement with the United States and probably saw merit in joining a more ample regional structure that could encompass other Latin American countries. We knew it would complicate negotiations somewhat but understood that politically it was a great step to show the relevance of the concept to all those sitting on the fence.

On the next day, February 6, the first hearings started in the Senate Finance Committee on the proposed negotiations, and that same month the International Trade Subcommittee of the House Ways and Means Committee held public meetings. The International Trade Commission, an independent agency, also held meetings on the subject in Phoenix, Chicago, and Washington, D.C. It was time to play ball. One of the important decisions Mexico had to make was to confront the political reality of having somehow to address environmental and labor issues in the debate. It was difficult because we thought we would be subject to all sorts of ill-intentioned harassment. To force the decision, I helped Jim Kolbe organize a public session for congressional staffers at the Longworth building. The program included presentations by Jaime Serra, Mexico's secretary of commerce; Timothy B. Atkeson, EPA assistant administrator for International Activities; and the deputy secretary of Sedesol, Sergio Reyes Luján, whose responsibilities included environmental protection. It was a risky decision, given the strong opposition in Mexico in some quarters; some believed that holding a session and discussing the issues would be tantamount to accepting them. I believed so strongly in the need for it that I stuck my neck out and said I would offer my resignation if things went wrong. We finally prevailed, and the program was held on March 21. From then on we were quite free to address those problems and not to dodge them, as we had to do earlier. This fateful decision lay the groundwork for actually winning the NAFTA vote and making NAFTA the greenest of all trade agreements.

Instead of focusing on the merits of free trade, the crucial debate became more of a side-show on labor problems, environmental risks, Mexico's record on human rights, and its political system. Given that the issues would not go away, the best possible decision was to approach them directly, hands on, as we had at the staffer forum. We brought high Mexican officials responsible for labor and the environment to the United States to address the issues. We were on solid ground: during the Salinas administration in October 1990—that is, before environmental problems in Mexico had become a concern in the U.S. NAFTA debate—a budget of $2.52 billion had been allocated toward resolving them, and more than 1,000 agreements had been signed with industries to install antipollution and emission control equipment. Even friends of Mexico were not aware that Mexican labor law and workers' rights frequently extend beyond what U.S. workers get—for example, generous maternity leave, no crossing of picket lines, et cetera.

Most important, congressional leaders also had to come to grips with the concerns by writing several letters to President Bush. Congressman Rostenkowski and Senator Lloyd Bentsen sent letters to the president very similar in content, urging him to consider environmental protection, health and safety standards in the workplace, and general workers' rights in Mexico. House majority leader Richard Gephardt wrote another letter on March 27 that extended to other issues, such as the need for worker retraining in the United States resulting from displacements caused by NAFTA and the need for monitoring human rights violations in Mexico. He touched on more strictly commercial points such as the need for strong safeguards to protect U.S. businesses threatened by Mexican imports and the need for strict rules of origin. Although we thought the letters, particularly Gephardt's, strong and demanding and regarded them somewhat uneasily, they paved the road for an affirmative vote. Gephardt in particular was going ahead of the issues of the moment and trying to influence the outcome of the negotiations themselves. President Bush promised an "Action Plan" to cover those concerns and in a response of May 1 addressed some of these issues, stating that both the United States and Mexico would look for appropriate solutions. He underlined the need to increase the labor and industry adjustment assistance foreseen in the trade adjustment assistance law for workers displaced as a consequence of trade competition from abroad.

We could not understand Majority Leader Gephardt. An obviously intelligent man, he is outwardly amiable and soft spoken but has great inner strength of purpose. His well-structured deliveries conceal the profound anticompetitive bias of his politics of envy. I was reminded of a friend who, referring to a Mexican politician, told me: "I know he is totally wrong. But he is so convincing." Gephardt played a big role during the fast-track vote and probably was the decisive element in the House—although I think Chairman Rostenkowski had to lean hard on him to leash his labor and human rights supremacist attitudes. His people told us, from the start, that at least 50 and probably 70 members would follow his lead on the vote. They may have slightly exaggerated, but we knew he was a man to reckon with. At times he made extremist statements that were softened by calls from his office telling us that what he really meant was slightly different and that we had to understand it within such and such context. He was like a moving target, zigzagging ahead and difficult to aim for at any particular moment but holding a very definite overall direction. I believed him to be totally impervious to our arguments and positions although he feigned understanding. Anyway, as a shrewd tactician with strong views yet smooth ways, he would continue during the side-agreement negotiations to play a considerable role. He would personally and repeatedly tell us that he was for a "fair and free" trade agreement. It all hinged upon the word "fair," the meaning of which was quite elastic as circumstances demanded but clearly connoted "managed" trade with protectionist undertones. This was his position in the failed "Gephardt amendment" and would continue to be his leitmotif. He was obviously very close to the trade unions, particularly in his district of St. Louis where they were rather powerful. I was extremely surprised to learn from actual citizens of St. Louis the extent of trade-union power there; in many cases belonging to a trade union ensured one a job, and paying dues to the union was adhered to almost as strictly as paying taxes. I could understand, because in certain respects there is a parallel to Mexican union traditions.

Opponents were forming coalitions of assorted groups. A "Mobilization on Development, Trade, Labor, and the Environment" was set up by 50 citizens' groups—labor, human rights, religious, consumer protection, and others. Joining the AFL-CIO and other trade unions were the Disciples of Christ Church, the Catholic Maryknoll Fathers, the Child Labor Coalition, Friends of the Earth, the Economic Policy Institute, and many other social and religious activists. They held a press conference at the National Press Club in Washington to release declarations opposing the fast track and proposing to expand the agenda of negotiations to include human rights, debt, child labor, and many other impossible dreams. They obviously had to have a sense that to overload the agenda was equivalent to killing the process. This was certainly their aim. I was surprised, however, to find that several of the individuals involved were dead serious, and their passionate radicalism was used—and abused—by the cold-hearted strategists that had put the whole together.

We had to recognize that support in the Congress was determined by the support of the people. Discussions of the fast-track procedure are not readily understood by most people, and free trade is an abstract concept for even the most alert. But the debate was being packaged in a manner that was resonating at the grass-roots level. The majority—close to 60 percent—of respondents to a national opinion poll conducted in April 1991 by Garin-Hart were either unfamiliar or slightly familiar with the proposal to enter into a free trade agreement with Mexico. But when given a choice of arguments for or against it, the respondents reacted strongly to those claiming it would hurt wages and living standards for U.S. workers. A high 58 percent thought it would help Mexico more than the United States. Fear-inspiring claims by the opposition were making inroads; the same poll showed 81 percent of the public thinking the economic situation to be unfavorable, which created a pessimistic attitude toward change that could be perceived as threatening. Nevertheless we could bank on a solid 46 percent who believed the net effect of the trade agreement to be favorable, as against 44 percent who regarded it as unfavorable.

We therefore had to focus on educating the public about the agreement's benefits, while urging other organizations to do the same, and we had to avoid being scared by unsubstantiated claims. We initiated a NAFTA tour around the country; after a mini-summit meeting with President Bush in Houston on April 7, President Salinas made visits to Boston, Chicago, San Antonio, and Austin. His main address, at Harvard University during the annual meeting of the American Society of Newspaper Editors, was a forceful statement about the "opportunity as seldom arises in history to decisively change the terms of a long, complex and unquestionable difficult relationship." He referred to the dramatic change in attitude in Mexico as a domestic process of modernizing its system and making the most of its relationship with its neighbors, which was "an undeniable geographical reality."

We targeted 31 U.S. media markets aimed toward influencing key undecided members of Congress. The tour events were coordinated by my office in Washington, D.C., with the assistance of Mexican Consulates and Mexico City Ministry of Commerce officials. Where possible we had the support of U.S. Department of Commerce officials and of local allies in the selected cities. Some events were canceled because of scheduling conflicts, but overall the tours were successful and were completed in the four weeks from early April to early May. At least 45 major news stories were published, as well as 30-odd positive editorials or opinion columns. We were learning fast. Certainly the whole project could not have been done without our lobbyists' orienting us toward which districts to target and the support of our public relations firm, Burson-Marsteller, whose personnel made the necessary appointments, distributed material, and advised us on the current problems in each area. Nevertheless, the cohesive energy of my Mexican team, working strenuously and operating like a platoon, was a great satisfaction. After three months we had been able to run a multifaceted campaign. Our organization began to be the subject of opposition attacks. These poor little Mexicans were creating mischief by abusing the sanctity of U.S. institutions and tolerance. This charge would become a major issue later during the negotiations and ratification process.

The role of the media became quite apparent during our first campaign in April–May. Members of Congress take national media coverage very seriously and regard local media reports in their own districts and states as key indicators of fluctuations in public opinion. Media influence was most important to us, given the abstract nature of "free trade." Although the principle strikes a positive chord with the average citizen, its contents are elusive and easily manipulated. Entrenched interest can be mobilized against a threat of change that engenders resistance. It is easier to single out a possible loss than to talk about the more general potential benefits that would be spread out across the country. And the prospect of losing one's job elicits a negative reaction much stronger than any positive response elicited by the possibility of new jobs. This was made rather clear to me at a session we had in rural Illinois with a group of congressmen and some major industrialists. One congressman, who represented a district with several broom factories, said his constituents were dead set against a Mexican trade agreement because they knew it would cause them to lose their jobs. A large industrialist countered: "We will have plenty of new jobs created by increasing Mexican business. Tell them to come to us if they are displaced." His statement, although absolutely correct, did nothing to deflect the opposition of the congressman, who weighed what he saw as a clear loss much more heavily than a potential benefit. Thus we put great effort into approaching the media and held meetings with editorial boards and reporters wherever we could. Forty-nine members of Congress were in the 22 media markets we visited on our tour, and most of them were either undecided or leaning against. By the end, nearly two-thirds ended up voting for fast-track extension.

The media are not monolithic, however. They displayed marked differences in attitude—if not necessarily in final positions—not only among different newspapers but among different functions of journalists as well. Editorial page editors tend to take a broader approach, even among those who are liberally inclined. U.S. newspaper editorials overwhelmingly supported and endorsed the fast track both at the national and local levels. Even renowned liberal newspapers like the *Washington Post* voiced strong and steady support—with 5 positive editorials preceding the fast-track approval.

News stories tended to be more mixed in their support, owing largely to the pride that U.S. reporters, many of whom are excellent in their preparation and analysis, take in exercising independent, balanced judgment. They tend to tell both sides of a story and have a certain proclivity to highlight strong news— which in our case was basically bad news.

We discovered several interesting trends in news reporting. Business reporters tended to produce stories reflecting predominant views of the pro-NAFTA business communities. Regional reporters tended to produce stories reflecting the predominant views in their areas on the likely effects on the local industry and jobs; because "all politics is local," they could highly influence members of Congress. We attempted to explain NAFTA's benefits for each of their regions by analyzing for them the local sectors that would most likely reap profits from it.

U.S. news stories out of Mexico tended to be investigative and more negative. In this type of journalism, what makes "news" is usually bad news. The prevailing prejudices and lack of understanding of Mexican culture and attitudes fostered by our opponents also emphasized the negative. TV stories tended to tilt toward the side that was holding a news event or the side that had produced or assisted in getting better pictures. Opponents here had the upper hand–for example, an AFL-CIO video of border pollution and working conditions was skewed toward making Americans terrified of the prospect of dealing in free trade with such a country. A crop of instant Mexico-specialists emerged. I was reminded of a conscientious professor who remarked: "Never write a book about a country you have not flown over at least once during the daytime."

The tremendous amount of news coverage certainly raised the importance of Mexico on the U.S. political and public agenda, but this had both positive and negative aspects. On the one hand it highlighted the radical market-oriented reforms of President Salinas, and on the other it highlighted Mexico's negatives by magnifying the perceived weaknesses of the environment, labor conditions, and the political system. Although the positive side outweighed the negative both during the fast-track stage and later before ratification, the Mexican financial crisis of 1995 gave the negatives a disproportionately high profile. After all, the crisis, albeit serious, would be short-lived, but the longer-term positive elements in the development of Mexican society would finally prevail.

The particular long-term views of editors or the short-term, local approach of reporters aside, what most interested the U.S. public was a simple, valid question: What is in it for us? The important thing was to talk about trade as prosperity and increased global competitiveness while at the same time stressing that environmental, health, and safety concerns, etc., would be adequately addressed.

Our Allies

In putting together the fast-track campaign, our team discovered the great potential of the U.S. Hispanic community. Accounting for 10 percent of the total population, Hispanic constituents could play a marginal but important swing-vote role in about 110 districts. They could be king-makers in those districts ranging from the traditional border states but spreading all the way to New Jersey, New York, and Illinois. In the past Mexico had certainly enjoyed good contacts with the community. During his 1989 visit to Washington, President Salinas met at Blair House with 10 of the most prestigious Hispanic leaders. Then, also, a section was created at the office of the secretary of foreign relations in Mexico, under Dr. Roger González de Cossío, to foster relations with the Mexican communities living abroad. This proved to be an extremely useful base.

Besides serving as swing-votes in certain districts, the Hispanics had two specific roles cut out for them. President Bush had to cull enough Democratic support for the fast track in spite of the opposition of two pillars of the democratic constituent groups—the unions and the environmentalists. The Hispanic community, which was traditionally democratic, emerged as a significant political factor in the political vacuum. This influence tended certainly to enhance the Hispanic community's role in social and political affairs in a country where they had been underrepresented. The most enlightened of its leaders clearly saw this. There was also a negative aspect that encouraged their participation—that is, their natural indignation at racist remarks and innuendos being spread by the opposition. They could not allow their traditions to be demeaned and thus took the opportunity to flex their muscles and be counted.

A special factor in their involvement was made clear to me at a cocktail party where many Hispanic leaders were present. An elderly local leader from Texas told me: "Sir, you make us proud of being of Mexican origin!" His eyes were warm and expressive. That evening, as luck would have it, I went back home and turned on the television. An old movie was showing—"Giant," whose very name suggests Texas. In the first, and only, scene I saw that evening, a family of poor, short Mexicans is being driven away from a small-town restaurant by an owner shouting that his restaurant is no place for them. The hero, a big Texan, obviously fights the owner, but the message is clear. I understood the deep meaning in the words of that old man. For him that scene must have been real.

Aware of their emerging political significance, the Bush administration started courting the Hispanic community and was intent on carving out a segment for the Republican Party. He fostered the creation of the Hispanic Alliance for Free Trade, led by Elaine Coronado; it reached out to many groups and was very useful in the process. But probably the most influential single Hispanic organization favoring the fast track was the National Council of La Raza, led by the thoughtful, clear-headed leader Raúl Izaguirre. Early on, he organized a trip to Mexico that included several other Hispanic associations in collaboration with my office and Dr. González de Cossío.

We had been certainly late in fostering this process and were still learning how to cope with the U.S. system. Our aim—to accomplish a united Hispanic voice in support of the fast track—was achieved with a Capitol Hill press conference on May 21, 1991. Several Hispanic congressmen were highly influential in this event—especially Bill Richardson, Solomon Ortiz, Kika de la Garza, Albert Bustamante, and Martin Frost. We held a cocktail party the evening before at the Mexican Cultural Institute on Sixteenth Street and were extremely happy to see among our guests Mr. Rafael Hernández Colón, the governor of Puerto Rico, who openly endorsed the fast-track proposal. In a strong letter to Speaker Thomas J. Foley, he stated, among other things, that "the expansion of trade . . . has been the engine for our economic growth and prosperity." Because we knew about the misgivings of some Puerto Rican groups, we worked hard to get their endorsement and were very pleased about his support, as well as the support of the representatives of the Cuban American Foundation. The most prominent of the other associations involved were "La Raza" and the Mexican American Legal Defense and Education Fund (MALDEF). We nevertheless failed to get the support of other important activist groups involved with the unions or with social activists like the "Southwest Voter Registration." The Hispanic influence in the vote was finally made clear in the 110 districts with a 10 percent proportion of constituents or more being of Hispanic origin. Sixty-three (63.1) percent of congressmen in those districts voted in favor of the fast track as against 53.5 percent of positive votes across all the districts.

We were encouraged by letters of support from several large, influential trade associations, who started collecting signatures and addressing them to members of Congress. They included the Chemical Manufacturers Association, Citizens for a Sound Economy, the Coalition for Open Markets and Expanded Trade or COMET (including the American Business Conference, which represents 100 of the largest, fastest growing corporations in the country), the American Farm Bureau Federation, the Food Processors, Manufacturers, Wholesalers, and Retailers, the Rail Shippers, the General Aviation Manufacturers, the Coalition for Trade Expansion, which included more than 360 large, successful companies, etc. We tried hard to maintain contact with these organizations, listened to their concerns and advice, and spoke frequently at their meetings. They had an obvious preference for Dr. Serra, a brilliant public speaker who received a good number of standing ovations and who occasionally had to accept me—at the last moment—as a replacement!

The Debate and the Vote

Research on the proposed free trade agreement was undertaken by several agencies, consulting firms, and think tanks. One of them was a solid study conducted by KPMG-Peat Marwick for the U.S. Council of the Mexico-U.S. Business Committee, which stated that the direct impact on the U.S. economy of removing trade barriers in Mexico would be positive but small overall because of the different sizes of the economies. The stimulus to investment, however—if adequately treated in the agreement—would be very great. The study addressed the specific impact on 44 business sectors. Its conclusions were just the kind of reasonable commonsense conclusions for which we were arguing. Research conducted under the auspices of the U.S. International Trade Commission (ITC) reached roughly the same conclusions. Touching on the contentious labor issue, it stated clearly that "an FTA is likely to have little or no effect on employment levels in the United States, but it could cause some shifts in employment among occupations. . . . the incentive for migration from Mexico to the United States will decline . . . real income for U.S. skilled workers and capital service owners is expected to rise . . . real income for unskilled workers in the United States is likely to decline slightly . . . total income in the United States would increase. . . . "[3] This was a fair conclusion pointing to the need for the United States to reinforce its worker adjustment training efforts, as demanded by noted members of Congress and agreed to by President Bush. Occasionally the game was played whereby research was misused, or interpretation of it was forced, to "prove" divergent conclusions. The initial draft of the ITC study had stated that unskilled U.S. workers would see a "slight" decline in real income. This was repeated ad nauseam – omitting the precious word "slight" in spite of later correction. But a worse case of misuse was the abuse of a study by Raúl Hinojosa, a California scholar. Jeff Faux of the Economic Policy Institute used the study to state that with a trade agreement the United States would lose 550,000 jobs. The author himself publicly announced that this was a distortion, because that figure represented a preliminary step based on rather restrictive assumptions.

The acrimony involved during the debate came as a shock to us because the debate involved only a concept: whether a free trade agreement with Mexico was in principle acceptable. A simple honest-to-God trade agreement, even with the inclusion of side issues, should fall within accepted U.S. traditions. Certainly Mexico's image was a significant impediment and would continue to be. Little did people appreciate Mexico's 30 centuries of art, the unparalleled greatness of the Toltec and Mayan traditions still at work in the country, and the great accomplishments of Spanish culture that developed an altogether different country from European values and Native American roots. Neither did people know about the substantial transformation, equivalent to a peaceful industrial revolution, Mexico had undertaken to modernize its economically and politically outdated systems. The image of Mexico as a poor, undereducated, undemocratic country frightened some people and became an issue in itself—if only by innuendo. One of our main tasks was to present Mexico as a country building a more promising future on its solid base of magnificent traditions.

A related problem, which we faced for the first time at this stage, was the difference in political styles in the United States and Mexico. The United States practices American-football-type political debate: tackle the enemy and smear him with mud if possible. The scenario had certainly changed from the smoke-filled rooms of yesteryear where decisions were made by a few notables and then proposed in whistlestop campaigns that had the spirit of a county fair. The Democrats had tried—in the aftermath of their Chicago convention during the Vietnam years and at a time when ubiquitous television emphasized the personality element—to make the system more open. The political landscape of the United States had become more radicalized on both extremes.

The Mexican style is rather like soccer where aggressive physical contact is penalized. The Mexican culture has certain "Asiatic" traits that may derive from the Asian origin of its first inhabitants: Mexican style is smooth and subdued in its expressions, courteous in its manners, and sometimes unfathomable—even to Mexicans. Delal Baer, a noted Mexicanologist, says that understanding Mexican politics is like analyzing shadows in a Platonic cave and trying to discover reality from them. The U.S. political system may be more brutal, but it is far more transparent.

Political transformation in Mexico is proceeding very quickly; by 1996 Mexican style had become far more strident than it was traditionally. Nevertheless, during the NAFTA process the Mexican political culture still retained many of its old characteristics. It could be compared with water-polo, where players always smile as they face the public even as they hit their opponents hard underwater. Odious discussion of the issues—U.S.-style—risked alienating Mexican support and even creating resentment and anti-Americanism. I personally was frequently involved in trying to "interpret" U.S. harshness to avoid unwarranted conclusions—that is, to help Mexicans understand that some statements made by U.S. politicians should not be taken at face value because their ideas are coined in harsher terms than Mexicans would use.

The end of May was the deadline for Congress to vote on renewing fast-track procedures aimed at concluding the Uruguay round of GATT and starting the NAFTA negotiations. President Bush's letter to the chairmen of the two Senate and House trade-related committees cleared the way for the fast-track vote by allowing both labor and environmental considerations to be included. It was Congress's turn then to vote. But some influential legislators believed a statement had to be made about the need to include these issues in the agreement and make future approval conditional on the fulfillment of certain points.

We learned that Chairman Rostenkowski and Majority Leader Gephardt were preparing a congressional resolution addressing these with the intent of stating the rules for the negotiations. We understood that the proposed resolution was too radical and got to talk to some of the committee staffers about it. This was of primary importance for Mexico, because a resolution with too many sharp teeth would make it impossible for Mexico—and Canada—to even initiate the negotiations. They would be overburdened to the extent that issues totally extraneous to trade—and even labor and environment—were being established as conditioning the whole. These included drug trafficking—certainly influenced by New York congressman Charles Rangel—human rights, and other issues. We were appalled. It would be a Pyrrhic victory. It would make things impossible to manage and would sink the boat with extra weight that did not belong there.

The issues were probably real, but the trade agreement was not the place to deal with them. We therefore had discussions with staffers and even got Secretary of Commerce Serra to personally join the effort. His engaging and powerful personality persuaded the drafters—the toughest of whom was Michael Wessel, Gephardt's chief of staff—to take a more nuanced approach.

This final version was finally accepted by both proponents and submitted to Congress for a vote as House Resolution 146, known also as the Gephardt resolution. In it Congress specified the trade and investment objectives that should be achieved in the negotiations and the environmental and labor-related goals to be pursued. Among other points, it indicated that NAFTA must permit the United States to provide adequate transitional safeguard measures to minimize dislocations, if any occurred. It insisted that NAFTA should permit the United States to maintain strict health and safety standards and that in carrying out the objectives of the presidential response of May 1 the president should seek to develop a joint program to address border environmental problems. The implementation of the agreement should be accompanied by an effective worker adjustment program that would be adequately funded and ensure that workers who lost their jobs as a result of the agreement would receive prompt, comprehensive services. The final draft also stated that the United States should be able to maintain its laws against injurious subsidies, dumping, and other unfair trade practices. We could live with those requirements, and the conditions were set for the case to go to the floor.

The final vote on the fast-track agreement took the form of a Dorgan bill in the House–which, to confuse the uninitiated, was established in terms of nonauthorization of the extension of the fast track–and in the form of the Hollings bill in the Senate. The vote was held on May 24. We Mexicans watched C-Span at our office on I Street with Dr. Herminio Blanco, the chief negotiator. We followed the vote count intensely. One congressman even voted no when he wanted to vote yes–meaning he wanted to vote no to the fast track but got it wrong as some of us did. He changed his vote. Finally the Dorgan bill was rejected–and therefore the fast track for both the Mexico and the GATT agreements was approved–by 231 votes against and 192 for. We had lost 65 percent of the democratic vote but had gained 67 percent of Republicans. In the Senate the approval of the fast track– meaning disapproval of the Hollings resolution–was passed by 36 votes against and 59 for. All in all, the outcome mirrored the political spectrum of the Congress with few exceptions, with the most welcome vote of Senator Ted Kennedy of Massachusetts in favor of the agreement.

But it was not over yet. On the same day Gephardt House Resolution 146 was voted on. It had been introduced by three initial sponsors on May 9–Richard Gephardt, Dan Rostenkowski, and Mel Levine–all Democrats. It included the president's verbal commitments but had been cleansed, as noted above, of the most audacious and inimical phrasing. The resolution was presented for a vote and approved by 329 votes for and 85 against. Although the resolution was meant as a nonbinding sense of the Congress, it accepted in principle the president's "Action Plan" and held him to it. The nays and ayes were rather clear as to their meaning. And their meaning was that an overwhelming majority in the House wanted NAFTA to be the greenest, most labor-friendly agreement yet negotiated. And so it happened, as will be seen.

Notes

1. At a later stage after the NAFTA passage, Mr. Kirkland retired under the pressure of this confrontation. Mr. Donahue, the heir apparent, was himself challenged by a rival of a "new" sort of union–the Services Employees Union. Donahue survived the challenge and was elected to replace Kirkland.

2. Pat Choate's article, "Can a Keiretsu Work?" in the *Harvard Business Review* (September 1990) is an excerpt from his book, *Agents of Influence* (New York: A. A. Knopf, 1990).

3. U.S. International Trade Commission, *Potential Impact on the U.S. Economy and Selected Industries of the North American Free Trade Agreement*, USITC Publication 2596 (January 1993).

2

The Negotiations

The negotiations started in June 1991. They covered practically all economic sectors, and the work was distributed to 19 different groups. Some subjects, like market access, applied to all exportable goods across an enormous variety of sectors. Market access was central to the agreement, because it not only involved the reduction of tariffs but defined the rules of origin. The rules really establish which goods are to be the beneficiaries of the NAFTA treatment by determining roughly the amount of value-added within the region that entitles them to special treatment. Thus a product with 60 percent regional content may be a regional product, but the exact same product with 50 percent value-added may not benefit from preferential treatment.

Other groups covered agriculture, financial services, transportation, investment, settlements of disputes, et cetera. The agreement proposed to discuss many subjects not generally considered in free trade agreements, such as agriculture and transfer of intellectual property. Although its scope was extremely ample, it did not fully establish an overall common market, mainly because migration was off limits—except for a few cases of temporary entry to provide professional services. A thorny aspect was energy because its inclusion was as important to the United States and Canada as its exclusion was to Mexico. It finally was included as a subgroup.

The negotiations developed at the ministerial, chief negotiator, and group levels. The groups met frequently, and after one or two rounds for each group, depending on the progress, a chief negotiator meeting was held. After an average of two such meetings, a ministerial session was scheduled to take stock, decide the remaining issues, and direct the next stage. The first ministerial meeting was held in Toronto, June 12, 1991, where the groups and the overall mechanics were established.

When the negotiations proper ended on August 12, 1992, 218,241 group meetings had occurred, 5 of which were plenary sessions held alternatively in the three different countries, and 2,710,465 phone calls had been made between the delegations. The chief negotiators met 11 times in formal sessions and the ministers met 7 times, including their final marathon meeting at the Watergate Hotel.

The progress achieved at the different groups was uneven, depending upon the political sensibility of each issue, its complexity, and the interplay of personalities involved. The most difficult subjects were energy, agriculture, and the auto industry, as well as issues related to dispute settlement—particularly antidumping.

The Stages

The negotiations developed in stages that in hindsight proved logical, but were neither planned or formalized as such. The first stage—"getting to know you"—consisted of trying to understand the basic nature of the other parties' position, while holding one's own position close to the chest. The problem was understanding. For instance, Mexican financial authorities rather tightly regulate financial institutions and their products, while the institutions themselves are allowed to provide a wide variety of financial services. In the United States, the tradition has been to limit specialized banking services but allow institutions great flexibility to create products for their markets—activity that is restricted in Mexico. To understand such diverse problems and traditions required a great effort, especially in the first stage. At times minor irritations ensued when an idiomatic expression, translated literally, seemed to convey a different meaning than was intended. A Mexican felt hurt when his U.S. colleague told him he would buy him a drink, which the Mexican understood as demeaning! Occasionally similar problems arose of a more serious nature, but all were resolved.

When the first barriers of communication and understanding were cleared, each delegation presented its requests and its restrictions and a second stage of negotiations ensued. Obviously the requests were outrageously demanding and the restrictions extremely defensive. These rigid positions constituted the most difficult part of the negotiations and in the fall of 1991 cast doubt on their future. A meeting at Lake Meech, close to Ottawa, should have lasted a whole day, but was dissolved in 15 minutes owing to the intransigence of both the U.S. and Mexican delegations. It was beautiful autumn weather, the Canadian wilderness gloriously adorned in red and gold maple leaves. Buses were to return in late afternoon to drive us back to Ottawa, but meanwhile we were stranded in an isolated, modest-sized mansion, embarrassed to speak to members of the other delegations and even finding it difficult to communicate within our own group. Because it was cold, even our walks in the forest had to be brief.

With the earlier stages of extreme demands and rigidities behind us, it was an opportune time for each delegation to take stock, clarify positions, and consider how the various parts fit together to ensure a logical whole. Thus also agreements and disagreements would be clearly identified. In October 1991, it was argued that every delegation should draft a comprehensive treatment, advances of which were exchanged in November. In a series of meetings at Georgetown University during January 1992, proposals were presented, and Mexico offered a first integrated text with columns comparing the positions of each country. A first "bracketed" text was developed that provided a framework for future discussions. Real problems were more easily focused, and futile controversies avoided in this, the third stage.

At Georgetown important strides were taken. U.S. chief negotiator Julius Katz showed flexibility, and the Mexicans were creative. The United States accepted certain Mexican positions on the auto industry, and the Mexicans relented on petrochemistry. Mexico was apparently ready to grant some points in investment and financial services, and the United States accepted a new concept for the textile industry.

The personality of Jules Katz was a good indicator of forthcoming negotiating weather. Because it is partly natural and partly his negotiating style for him to appear hard, any signs of flexibility on his part would be noticed. And those signs were present. We had achieved some consensus in particularly difficult matters and had a common text—although nearly every paragraph was interspersed with brackets that included the diverging positions of the countries involved. A fourth stage began that would last for months; we would be engaged in discussing the common text and "debracketing" or getting specific agreements on divergent ("bracketed") positions.

Obviously the most difficult issues remained bracketed the longest, and the intervention of ministers became more necessary at each further step. The common bracketed text concept was deceiving and probably helped raise the conflicting issues to the forefront—the "discussion-breaking" points. But it clarified the sticking points that would require difficult political decisions.

The different styles, cultural backgrounds, strategic positions, and conflicting interests defined the personalities of each delegation during the whole period. Mexico started with the weakest position, Canada with the strongest. Not only did the Mexican delegation have the least experience in trade negotiations, given Mexico's economic isolation, but it represented by far the weakest and least developed economy with many internal disequilibria. Politically it had the most to gain because NAFTA would give its modernization process powerful thrust. Moreover, President Salinas had departed from commonly held traditions, and Mexico had more to lose, as registered in the nervous reactions of the Mexican stock market during the negotiations. It had the greatest sensitivity to the whole concept and would have to pay the highest cost in adjusting to the competition that would be unleashed with a successful outcome of the negotiations.

The main elements of the Mexican position were clear to the delegation. Previous research and analysis by different social groups had thoroughly detailed the strengths and weaknesses of the Mexican economy and provided a clear idea of what Mexico wanted. Our objective was to maximize political support in the United States at minimal political cost in Mexico. Enough concessions had to be made to create a network of support in Congress and the private sector.

The issues had to be addressed within the context of an economic recession, which makes people fearful, and the changed global position of the United States. Paradoxically, the United States had won the Cold War and shown its systems to be more adequate to solving economic problems, but had lost a clear sense of direction and moral rectitude in its foreign policy. Also, U.S. capitalism thrives in competition, but doubts about U.S. competitiveness—to a large extent unfounded—were pervasive, especially in relation to Japan and Germany. In effect, such doubts strengthened protectionistic attitudes and bolstered the search for other ways to acquire competitiveness through regionalization of the economy.

The negotiations were unorthodox. The Mexican government on its own and apart from any negotiation considerations would have made some of the changes toward modernization that it also used as bargaining chips. The Americans were sometimes at a loss to know whether they were pushing for something the Mexicans themselves already wanted but were using as a negotiating tool.

The Style

The negotiations proceeded within the context of different "styles" of playing politics and running personal discussions. The organization and management of the whole process was centralized for Mexico and departmentalized for the United States. Because the subjects to be negotiated cut across different sectors of each country's administration, representatives from all of them participated. Nevertheless, in the case of Mexico, persons responsible for each group were part of the Office for the Free Trade Agreement headed by chief negotiator Herminio Blanco. For the United States, usually the persons most responsible belonged to the corresponding agencies, with the USTR playing an overall coordinating role. Once again Mexico was relying on the idea of a task force totally focused upon the achievement of a goal.

Other style differences surfaced: the Mexican side tended to concentrate all information at the top whence came directives to the different groups that knew little about the progress made in other groups. The U.S. system produced a variety of leaks both planned as an overall strategy and accidental (or deriving from special interests), whereas in Mexico a tight operation foreclosed any informal disclosures. This difference meant that decisions were more easily arrived at by Mexico. Secretary of Commerce Jaime Serra had direct and immediate access to President Salinas as well as to the different ministries involved in the processes. When decisions were due, the machinery was there to provide them. In the case of the United States, the more decentralized system took more time for positions to be arrived at and decisions taken.

Initially, each group started using its own language with the help of simultaneous translation to communicate with participants of other groups, which proved cumbersome. Participants often had to correct translators, and wasteful repetitions occurred. All Mexican participants had an adequate command of English, and thus finally English was used in all private sessions despite fears it could be badly interpreted in Mexico. (An opponent had chastised negotiators as people who "speak in English and think in English," meaning their concepts were alien to Mexican culture.) Such was the style—hands-on practical solutions to otherwise intractable problems. A delegation should be proud that it can command another language, a skill that gives it high standing vis-à-vis others who cannot or will not do the same.

The United States was guided by an insistence on general principles that would then be applied to actual problems. This is consonant with U.S. foreign policy traditions based on moral principles in the Wilsonian spirit as against the European balance of power—realpolitik. And although the Wilsonian spirit has been dead for a long time—and never lived to see an official day in the United States—its idealistic underpinnings continue as part of the U.S. outlook, especially during the Cold War. At times foreigners interpret the U.S. position as simple bullying and throwing weight around under a mantle of righteousness, but some of it originates in a competitive U.S. spirit, which is often perceived as greed – for money and power. Also, U.S. weight in world politics has produced a big brother attitude of imposing principles. By contrast, the Mexican approach was to seek trade-offs and accommodation in a "sectoral balance of economic interest." Mexico preferred a case-by-case approach to problem-solving and therefore clashed on occasion with its counterparts. An element in the "general principles" area that the Mexican delegation willingly adopted was the need for procedural transparency because it very much fitted with its intention to develop a more open government and society.

Mexico's regulatory system allowed great latitude for interpretation by government agencies (somewhat against the traditions of the Roman-Napoleonic civil law). This nondemocratic element gave too much discretionary authority, but has provided a great flexibility in political adjustment. Although it was undergoing transformation during the process of Mexico's modernization, it was still there, tainting Mexican approaches to regulations and leading to some difficulties in comparing norms and regulations among the countries.

Mexico's negotiators were a new breed, dissatisfied with the old tradition of allowing too much interpretation in their desire for a country disciplined by law. During the whole process Mexico accepted clear unambiguous norms and the existence of general principles whose logic – like the ones relating to monopolies – would cut across several sectors that the government in the past had kept as a restricted domain. This process forced definitions that have had – and will continue to have – a positive impact in the efficiency and the accountability of the Mexican system. Ironically, Mexico actually did strive for these values and was fighting a domestic battle against the forces aiming at conserving the status quo.

On one occasion in Washington, almost at the end of the side-agreement negotiations, I went out for dinner with Secretary Serra and chief negotiator Blanco to a cozy restaurant serving oriental food. In a relaxed mood because we could see the end approaching, our conversation wandered away from the negotiations to related issues. I asked the secretary which were in his opinion the most important noneconomic benefits of the agreement. To my enormous satisfaction, he readily answered: "This will help make Mexico a better and more just country." He was thinking about the disciplines of transparency that converged with our thinking about the need for more accountability in the system.

Personalities played a big role. In some cases both the U.S. and Mexican heads of groups understood each other's objectives and limitations and with hard work and respect made great progress in rather complex issues, such as market access or the textile industry. Other issues dragged on a long time, crippled more by a lack of chemistry between the personalities involved than by the subject itself. The auto industry, for example, included the "cultural" problem of understanding the convoluted complexity of the Mexican auto industry regulations. Obviously the personalities that were most clearly involved in the whole process and that most influenced the final outcome were those of the ministers—Jaime Serra, Mike Wilson, and Carla Hills—and of their chief negotiators, Herminio Blanco, John Weeks, and Jules Katz.

Dr. Serra, a highly energetic person, tends to create an atmosphere of excitement wherever he is. It always surprised me to watch him at work. The night before ministerial meetings, we would hold a briefing session for him. He immediately grasped the issue at hand and got involved in deciding what positions to take and which strategy to follow. He produced a continuous stream of creative ideas but kept an open mind to listen to other positions. The next day, as negotiations started, he addressed the issues with the command of someone who had been working at them continuously for a long time. He changed the rhythm when it suited him and played with ease and charm. His enthusiasm, grasp of intricate problems, decision-making ability, and tactical maneuvering amazed me. He was a man his counterparts could not hate and frequently enjoyed his theatrical use of the negotiating table as a stage.

Dr. Herminio Blanco was the real craftsman of the agreement from the Mexican side. His clear intelligence, tremendous hard work, and smooth manner of conducting the negotiations were outstanding. Nobody—in any delegation—had such a grasp of complex issues, such a knowledge of detail, and such a sense of mission. He worked assiduously, was a hands-on, sometimes secretive, manager but always open to ideas and creative. At times in the tension before the morning negotiations began, one could feel a cold shiver in the room as the delegations came together. Dr. Blanco would enter with an easy smile on his face, and the atmosphere would change. He rarely lost his temper, although he would have had ample opportunities, and maintained his lucid calm and warmth. Sometimes he would come out with his disarming, "Now, Jules, don't give me that . . . ," which made people, even Jules himself, smile and relax.

Blanco's deputy and head of the Mexico City office was Jaime Zabludovsky, without whose enduring, intelligent support things would not have proceeded as smoothly. His great sense of responsibility combined with sound judgment frequently put runaway discussions back on track. And the light touch of his elegant sense of humor lent great relief to tense and sometimes exhausting situations.

I did not know the U.S. and Canadian negotiators very well but came to appreciate them a lot. Carla Hills struck me as a "crystal lady" (as compared with former British prime minister Margaret Thatcher, the "iron lady"). Her clear understanding of the issues combined with an elegant, composed manner balanced the sometimes temperamental displays of Dr. Serra. She was a refined and always delightful person to deal with. Her lawyer's mind was sharp at analyzing arguments but was therefore slow at reaching conclusions. She was more trial lawyer than judge. But her firm clarity was evident, and she greatly contributed to the final balanced outcome and was personally and forcefully involved in breaking through several impasses.

Jules Katz was a most honest and difficult opponent. You would start by hating him, then proceed to respecting and finally liking and admiring him. He brought considerable negotiating experience to the table and knew when to brag, when to concede, when to play a weak hand with a poker face, when to be unremitting and demanding with his face blushing into a vivid red. His honesty was always apparent as he discussed things in a serious manner. Although strong tempered at times, he was never discourteous. He was a man whom his superiors and his opponents could trust.

His deputy Charles ("Chip") Roh, a man with a sharp mind and light touch, was always forthcoming and helpful in the myriad little or big items involved. He was ready to look for creative solutions and understood the Mexican positions in a very balanced way. His delightful humor comforted us frequently in the form of caricatures and cartoons on subjects that he circulated around the table to the merriment of all.

In my position, I had little contact with the Canadians. Suffice it to say that the balanced perspective of John Weeks, the chief negotiator, always helped to get things back on track. A stable, smiling, and somewhat timid person, he was an honest broker and at times a forceful advocate of his country's positions.

Funny things occasionally happened. When discussing the capital goods industry, Jaime Serra remarked, "Imagine Carla, when you get a $1 billion market in Tabasco!"—referring to the Mexican state of Tabasco where much of the oil industry is located. Carla Hills replied, "Now, come on, Jaime, don't you think that is a lot of Tabasco sauce?" Once when discussing imports of wood into Mexico, Dr. Serra pointed to the size of the Mexican market that would be purchasing so many metric tons from the United States. Carla said, "But Jaime, that is worth four hours work for that industry in the United States" to which he retorted: "Well, Carla, but think about the rate of growth!"

On another occasion, we were meeting in Mexico in the beautiful countryside of Oaxtepec, close to Cuernavaca. It was morning, and dark grey clouds began to cover the skies. Suddenly, rapidfire popping noises exploded close-by. The Americans and Canadians shivered and looked around in dismay, thinking surely a group of bandidos was besieging us or a civil war had started. We had some trouble explaining that Mexican farmers burn firecrackers as a defense against threatening hail during the rainy season. So much for cultural misunderstanding.

The Balance

How to achieve balance was a key issue, especially for the Mexican delegation. The problem leaked into many discussions. What sort of balance was appropriate? Certainly it was not that concessions within each sector had to be balanced. But even overall balance was extremely difficult to define, because we were considering countries with great disparity in their economic maturity. What was then the meaning of balance in such a case? To complicate things even further, Mexico was a newcomer to free trade. It had belatedly entered the GATT and, as such, had the prerogative of holding its tariffs at a high 50 percent average, although it had set them much lower. The process of eliminating a Mexican tariff of, say, 20 percent as against a prevailing U.S. tariff of 5 percent in 10 years created a much heavier burden of adjustment on Mexico.

Mexico wanted its status as a developing country recognized and integrated into the balance, which was finally achieved by allowing Mexico a slower start in tariff reduction. Thus, whereas almost 80 percent of Mexican exports to the United States were tariff free from day one, only 41.1 percent of U.S. exports to Mexico were to be free on the same date. The bulk of Mexican reductions would come at a later stage with 19.3 percent in five years time and 37.7 percent in ten years. The problem of balance surfaced at every stage until, at the ministerial meeting of Zacatecas, the decision was reached to analyze equilibrium at the end. Yet at different stages a highly "unbalanced" sectoral agreement developed. In the financial industry, for instance, U.S. firms are allowed much more latitude in Mexico than Mexican firms in the United States—although they have always been free to enter the United States and therefore all "concessions" were on the part of Mexico. As mentioned earlier, the United States already has a differentiated financial system with investment banks and commercial banks not permitted in principle to intrude into each others' markets and a fragmented structure of state and national banks and various regulations as to branch banking. Mexico, on the other side, has an integrated financial system at both the functional and national levels. Any concessions by Mexico meant a wider opening than in the case of the United States. But obviously Mexico would profit more than the United States from this "unbalanced" concession. Thus the problem of attaining a balance at a sectoral and a national level among such diverse economies was a rather tricky problem that would haunt us for a long time.

The balance sought was, in the words of a Canadian participant, "not an arithmetic but a political balance." Mexico had to make enough concessions to provide the U.S. private sector an incentive to support the agreement in the U.S. Congress. The United States had to avoid trying to impose unacceptable conditions on Mexico.

The position of each country had many inconsistencies because each was trying to achieve freer trade and investment flows in the most protective way possible. At one time during the negotiations, a U.S. participant said, "It is impossible to couple free trade with an infant industry argument"—that is, the Mexican position on the capital goods industry very much depends on government contracts. (According to the infant industry theory, a government should protect its infant industries from import competition until they can mature and become competitive.) But similar expressions could be used to describe inconsistent U.S. positions in the maritime industry, peanut butter, or apparel, although the epithet "infant" would be scarcely applicable.

This was a two-edged sword in each country's case. Mexico, wanted fiercely to keep Pemex—the state-owned oil monopoly—out of the discussions for constitutional reasons, but was then forced to put on the table purchasing agreements of Pemex's (and of other large parastatal groups) that had been utilized as a "set-aside" to promote the Mexican capital goods industry. Thus finally Mexico—with some rather important limitations—let its "set-asides" go. In the case of the United States, the prevalent set-asides are geared to help foster the entrepreneurial spirit of ethnic minorities, and obviously they could not be allowed to be negotiated. (Later, after the victory of Republicans in Congress, these very set-asides have met with some efforts to dispose of them, or at least restrict them.)

The interests of Mexico as potential supplier to the U.S.

government, given her economic status, was in the opening of precisely those U.S. sectors that were "set aside." By opening its parastatal sector's procurement to its trading partners, Mexico was in fact opening the largest share of government procurement of interest to foreign suppliers. By including local and state government procurement, it was opening itself in a very unbalanced way. Because the United States does not have a large "parastatal" sector to speak of, there was little to do there. The most interesting governmental sectors in the United States from a Mexican point of view—that is, purchases and ethnic set-asides yielding a market more akin to Mexico's capabilities—were closed. Beyond this the United States interprets its "national security" concepts rather broadly to include such mundane items as uniforms for soldiers as "set-asides" of a nonethnic character, and many other things a layman would not consider essentially pertaining to it. A real sectoral balance was in this case impossible, but an approximation was achieved by allowing Mexico to set aside from international bidding an important amount—which it would probably use to sustain the development of its capital-goods industry. Thus sectoral imbalances had to be regarded in the context of overall balance.

The Mexican negotiators conscious of the weakness of their country were initially most defensive and tried to win small skirmishes in different sectors rather than accepting sweeping principles from which unpleasant and unacceptable consequences could be derived. The perceived weakness of Mexico forced the Mexican team into a full-time, full-speed operation. Negotiators worked long daily hours, with scarcely a free weekend, to prepare for all possible contingencies. Like Avis, they worked harder because they were second, or in this case third, best. The strategy was to cover everything. It was a "carpet bombing" style of shooting at anything that moved—or could cause any trouble.

As a result, by doing that the Mexicans became highly competent in all the issues concerned. After the negotiations ended, by chance I encountered Jules Katz on an airplane flight. After we began to reminisce on the crucial points in the negotiations, I asked him what things had impressed him most. Without giving it much thought, he answered: "The development of the Mexican team." They had initially perceived the Mexicans as insecure who could be easily manipulated, he explained, but as negotiations proceeded they came to appreciate the quality and professionalism of their counterparts. This respect—certainly justifiable because I knew the great efforts of the Mexican team and the successes it had accomplished—greatly contributed to bringing NAFTA to a successful conclusion.

The Substance

The substance of and extent of the agreement can be grasped easily when reviewing the index of chapters, appendixes, and annexes of the agreement itself. They range from market access to investment, and lengthy annexes define the limits and restrictions for the three countries.

The end result of negotiations pertaining to free trade is derived from the free trade model that underpins the whole concept. Thus, to a certain extent the substance of the agreement was known in advance as an ideal. But this had to be approached within a number of economic and political restrictions that blurred the final outcome but finally made it and its provisos possible. In the case of Mexico, an added element came into play during the whole process—that is, the ongoing transformation of Mexican society from a state-oriented to an efficient market-oriented system. Thus, although to a certain extent the final image of the negotiations was present from the start, the collecting, defining, and fitting together of the puzzle pieces was an enormous task.

During the fast-track stage, Mexico, particularly its Washington-based team, had made a great effort to forge alliances with the U.S. private sector, making friends with members of Congress and establishing important links with the Hispanic communities in the United States. The very nature of the negotiations forced a change in the relations that had been generated. Our friends were, so to speak, seated at the other side of the table. The most important task now was to gather intelligence on the possible positions of the U.S. delegation and the political support involving them. But this had to be done more by the analyzing of issues and conditions than by the actual lobbying of the previous stage.

With the benefit of hindsight, the various issues involved can be categorized as conceptually divisive (energy and the dispute settlement arrangements); technically difficult (the automotive sector); politically problematic (agriculture and glass); or tactically important for the whole process (foreign investment and finance).

Another way to consider the different issues was by international or local orientation, degree of foreign participation, and the amount of direct political activity of the sectors involved. Firms with a large international exposure and plants in many countries tend to consider the whole as a market to be supplied by the most rationally efficient production system possible. These firms, like the household appliances industry, tend to favor free trade and the least restrictions possible. On the other hand, locally oriented firms can have an outlook over the whole territory of a country, such as the retail sector for apparel. They tend to look not so much for free trade but for the cheapest possible sourcing. In this case, with some provisos, they tended also to support NAFTA. Other sectors tend to have a heavy regional concentration in a certain territory comprising a limited number of states, as is the case of the textile or the glass industry. They have a proclivity toward protectionism or, if they do not feel threatened, toward forcefully opening other markets. Some of them also have great political clout facilitated by their regional concentration.

Sectors that have a sizeable foreign participation are oriented toward a broader market and production concept and thus included firms supporting free trade concepts, or at least not heavily on the opposing side. Such was the case of the cosmetic and the dyes sectors. Their importance overall was minor, though.

Because political activism varies in degree from sector to sector, it was difficult for us to ascertain an underlying overall logic to it. It is related to many elements such as historical traditions, dependency from government in law-making or regulatory capacity (like the pharmaceutical or the shipping sectors), or simply purchasing force. Regional concentration tended to give those sectors too much political weight. At times it was simply a will to promote the sectors' fortunes through political means. One of the most important means is the use of PACs sponsored by corporations, trade unions, and trade associations that contribute heavily–although in restricted ways–to candidates' campaigns. Out of the 20 largest PACs, 11 were sponsored at the time by trade unions, ranging from the Teamsters as the most important one to the Brotherhood of Carpenters, the United Auto Workers, or the International Association of Machinists.

Initially we tried to gauge how important different sectoral and industry interests were for individual members of Congress to help us determine a strategy for the concessions we were bound to make in order to get the necessary number of votes. The original plan was to create a matrix with the positions of the most important members of Congress on all the topics to be discussed during the negotiations. It was a typically technocratic scheme like an econometrics model, but it proved impossible as the necessary information was beyond our reach, and it would have been useless anyhow. Only a limited number of issues are of interest to different congressmen, because no one can follow them all. In many cases members become interested in an issue only just before it comes up for a vote, and many either defer their positions to the opinions of members they trust on a particular problem or abide by the leadership's recommendation. In the end we achieved the same results by analyzing which items (that is, airplanes, apples, glass, steel) were most relevant to the 40 most important opinion leaders in Congress. This scheme helped enormously in determining our position on different items.

The Contents

One of NAFTA's main achievements was to broaden market access: it provides for tariffs to be eliminated within 10 years' time for the vast majority of goods. After it takes account of the problem of balance between countries at different stages of economic development as mentioned above, 98.5 percent of Mexican tariffs on U.S. goods will be eliminated within 10 years, while 98.7 percent of U.S. tariffs imposed on Mexican goods will be eliminated during the same period, and Canadian tariffs facing Mexico will go down 99.0 percent. Further, the existing tariff structure is rather unbalanced and protective. Thus Mexico faced especially high tariffs for 252 of its products, 70 percent of which would be eliminated by the year 2000. Examples are watermelon, which faces a U.S. tariff of 35 percent, and asparagus (25 percent).

Nontariff barriers are also eliminated, providing national treatment to goods from the other member countries, except such items as used machinery for Mexico and national security for the United States. National treatment obviously means non-discrimination, and there are many ways special interests have been able to protect their markets. Many of them are addressed in the agreement, although exceptions are allowed in sensitive sectors.

Rules of origin are defined to ensure that the benefits of the agreement be granted only to goods originating within the region. Several creative elements not found in other agreements were devised and widely used, such as the change in tariff nomenclature and the use of invoice value as against a more prevalent and cumbersome "net cost" valuation. In particular, a change in tariff nomenclature works like this: are Mexican tortillas made with Australian corn eligible as regional goods? In the tariff schedule, the appropriate heading 1901 states that inputs considered in any other chapter except chapter 4 are admissible as proof of regional origin. Thus tortillas are Mexican even if made out of Australian corn because corn is not included in chapter 4, which implies there is enough regional value-added in the process to justify such a treatment.

No one should be surprised that agriculture was one of the most difficult subjects to deal with. It always is. In almost every country, agriculture is the most protected of economic activities because farmers usually wield great political power and evoke sympathy from the people. After all, they represent the country's traditions and provide its basic needs. A special problem arose because overall balance was difficult to achieve. If Mexico sought concessions on farm products in return for Mexican concessions in nonfarm sectors, it would meet with strong opposition of farm-bloc members of Congress. But people are ready to make concessions that do not exact a price, so Mexican concessions on farm products in return for U.S. concessions on nonfarm products with less political clout would be possible in the minds of the farm bloc but scarcely achievable. The strongest support in Congress was for the sugar industry—which case became a cause célèbre during the last days of the ratification process—and for tomato, asparagus, avocado growers, and tobacco and peanuts as well. Also politically sensitive was the citrus industry, for which an additional letter of understanding was adjoined to the agreement before ratification.

In NAFTA, it was impossible to write a single chapter for agriculture. Instead, three agreements ensued: a chapter on agriculture included in the U.S.-Canada Trade Agreement, and two chapters for the U.S.-Mexico and Canada-Mexico agreement. The latter excludes the elimination of tariffs and quotas for dairy products, poultry, eggs, and sugar. Most of this was due to the great political influence of Quebec at a time when the Ottawa government did not want to push the French province around.

Poultry presented special problems. In the United States, the industry tends to be located in the region that comprises Maryland, Virginia, and North Carolina. Regional issues tend to have more political clout because of the industry's proportionally higher participation within the districts and influence on the interests of members of Congress. Further, the main corporations in the industry maintained active lobbying operations in Washington, and Frank Perdue, the most illustrious of the industry figures, was a major GOP fundraiser.

At issue were phytosanitary standards for poultry and interpretation of the 1989 Farm Bill's statement that countries wishing to ship processed chicken to the United States must have inspection standards equal to those of the United States. What did "equal" mean? We thought the term "comparable" or "technically equivalent" should adequately cover the meaning instead of "exactly the same as" (if the United States keeps water at 36 degrees, for example, the foreign producer has to do the same).

This scheme was obviously protectionist, and the phytosanitary arrangement would finally prescribe discriminatory measures and admit equivalent measures only on a scientific basis.

The transition period of up to 15 years was the longest in the agreement if we abstract from minor elements like used vehicles that have a longer period. This was applied to corn, beans, powdered milk, and dried onions in the case of Mexican restrictions, and of peanuts, sugar, concentrated orange juice, broccoli, and asparagus on the U.S. side. For the most difficult cases, tariff rate quotas (TRQs) were used to establish a certain tariff-free amount above which a good is subject to a rather high rate. During the transition the quotas increase as the tariffs decline so as to be totally free at the end of the period.

The products with the longest transition periods were the most difficult to negotiate—particularly sugar and citrus, as shown later in a discussion of the eleventh-hour debate before the vote in Congress. These products were not important for their economic weight in the economy but because of their strategic position on the political spectrum for the United States and Canada. In the case of Mexico it was vitally important to more than 2 million farmers that the transition for corn and beans be treated adequately because a great proportion are traditional farmers with comparatively low productivity and would otherwise be subject to devastating pressures.

Mexico's rather complicated land tenure system has played a strong, dramatic role in the country's history. Zapata was only the most noted among rebels who raised the banner of land ownership for the poor peasant and the village communities. Mexico's three-tiered land tenure system has consisted of private property, communal property, and the *ejido*. The ejido is a peculiar type of communal property that originated from the Indian culture and was later preserved and developed by the Spanish government. Every ejido consists of a sizable property owned by the nation but assigned for use to a number of ejido members who work the land either individually or collectively. Its operation has long been subject to many restrictions. Not an actual property, it cannot be sold or mortgaged, which makes the financing of production a risky undertaking accomplished at high losses by government entities. An ejido could not rent out a parcel of its land or enter a business association with adjoining private farmers. Private property has been subject to many restrictions on maximum size and has been liable to incursions by ejido land claims of neighboring peasant townships who had the right to be granted the use of an ejido. The communal lands, the third type of land tenure, are the actual property of a village community and are under fewer restrictions; they are not widely used except in the northern states.

Further, varied subsidies were granted to different crops, and official prices were dictated for the most important. Every year new prices were fixed at which the Conasupo–a government agency that financed and bought agricultural products–would buy. The exercise created artificial bounty for some crops, misery for others, and great uncertainty for all. This seriously inefficient system required deep surgery, which it received during the same period that the NAFTA agreements were being negotiated.

The agreements in the agricultural sector were thus coupled with profound reforms in the Mexican system that took into consideration, at least partially, the principles established under NAFTA. The structures of subsidies to agriculture were revamped, simplified, and made neutral in their differential impact (the "Procampo" system). The communal land tenure system (the ejido) was freed from the strict rigidities that the former law defined. Farmers were set free to produce what would be more economically convenient, and ejido members were allowed to choose the land tenure system most congenial to their interests and traditions, whether private or their old one, but with fewer restrictions than before. The basic elements were thus established to incorporate traditional agriculture into a modern system.

Another traditional sector that has historically been protected is textiles and apparel. In the United States, for example, 125 categories in that sector were subject to quotas with tariffs as high as 57 percent. In the case of Mexico 40 percent of imports from the United States were subject to tariffs at a 20 percent level. Mexico is a relatively small exporter to the United States of these items, which comprised at that time a little less than a third of the U.S. imports from China.

Opposing interests have prevailed in the U.S. textile industry. On the one hand, the "Crafted with Pride in the USA Council" had since 1985 spent $100 million in its "Buy American" campaign. Its most important sponsor was Roger Milliken, a millionaire textile industrialist. On the other hand, many apparel retailers—such The Gap, Warnaco, and The Limited—had international connections. It was crucial for Mexico to define its own alternative choices. If the agreement finally established a simple transformation, moving from cloth to apparel as defining regional content, we would loose the heavy capital-intensive textile industry, but could gain investment and lower-skilled employment. If we went the way of triple transformation—meaning that the original fiber had to originate in the region—we would not expect that much of a light investment but could have as a strategy the rational integration of the whole industry in the North American region. We had to choose, given the political influence of the different groups, either to try to promote light investment and employment in Mexico or to get more votes in Congress with a concept of regional integration. With a triple transformation, we could get 40 to 45 votes of the textile caucus, but lose probably 12 votes on the retail side of the business. The decision was for the triple transformation and establishing the basis for regional integration of the textile industry. Yet protectionism is an attitude rather than rational estimation, and Roger Milliken continued to oppose NAFTA and to finance the likes of Buchanan or Perot's "United We Stand." Nevertheless, when the opinions really counted, the majority of the textile caucus in the House—56.3 percent—voted in favor of NAFTA.

The changes were also sweeping and important to the world trade in textiles because, in contrast to the multifiber agreement now in operation, NAFTA set a new style of facing difficult problems still subject to special quota-related agreements. In NAFTA quotas are eliminated for all originating articles after scheduled transition periods, which for the majority of products end by the year 2000.

Canada took some exceptions in the apparel industry in the case of nonoriginating products because it has a high fashion industry closely connected to foreign, nonregional imports.

Perhaps the most contentious issue was energy. As Mexico was well aware, several groups in the United States had made the assurance of energy supplies an important condition for entering into the agreement, and the energy issue was of highest interest to the U.S. government. The United States wanted Mexico to provide assurance of energy (petroleum) supplies in case of an emergency. The Canadian free trade agreement had provided such assurances, and the United States did not see why Mexico would not do the same. We knew that important concessions in this sector would pave the way for eventual ratification in the U.S. Congress. Mexico was caught in a dilemma. The energy sector, comprising oil, gas, electricity, and nuclear energy, was by constitutional mandate under state control. No exploration and exploitation of petroleum or natural gas and their distribution and sale can be conducted except by the Mexican government, and, with minimal exceptions, power generation, distribution, and sale was also its exclusive right.

Further, the energy sector had become part of a nationalistic myth. In its fight for independence from foreign domination – U.S. as well as European – the expropriation of oil companies in the 1930s had become a landmark that was celebrated politically as a great achievement.

A crucial element was also the obsolescence of much of the energy sector and the need for financial resources and technology to develop it into what it was proclaimed to be – a support to the country's independent development. Mexico was therefore pushed by domestic legal, political, and business considerations and U.S. and Canadian pressure to open the sector to foreign investment. The U.S.-Canada Free Trade Agreement provided that Canada would consider the importance of energy supplies to the United States in an emergency as equal to its own domestic needs. This was nevertheless abhorrent to Mexican political and social feelings and became a sore point for Canada, which apparently had given up on something a weaker country would not.

Initially, energy did not even merit a negotiating group among the original groups. But the problem would not fade away and thus was discussed discreetly and defensively by Mexico, whose policy came to be defined as follows: (1) no obligation to guarantee petroleum supplies; (2) no investment in areas reserved to the Mexican state; (3) no free trade in the energy sector reserved to the state; (4) no risk contracts in the energy sector; and (5) no foreign gasoline stations.

The energy sector entailed the existence of other monopolies managed by the government apart from the ones covered under the Mexican "no's." The production and distribution of gas was by law a monopoly as was the generation and distribution of electricity. Pemex, the national oil company, owned several subsidiaries in the petrochemical sector now open to private investment. Illegitimate and unfair competition could result if Pemex were a supplier of basic feedstuff for both its own and privately owned plants and provided the former with favorable conditions. It was therefore decided that transparency would be the standard and that Pemex in its dealings with its own subsidiaries should subject itself to prevailing market conditions.

Another problem—the preference given to Mexican capital goods producers that supplied the oil industry—was also addressed in the procurement articles discussed later. From the beginning of the negotiations, the energy sector was paradoxically both conspicuously absent and permanently present. It was touched upon in several other group discussions and was the subject of continuous, largely unfounded, rumors in the Mexican press.

The Americans, although virtuously discreet to the outside, were unremitting in their will to force the issue to debate and to condition it on agreement in other areas. Jules Katz, the chief U.S. negotiator, was particularly blunt and persistent to the point of abruptness on the subject and frequently noted the perceived inconsistency of the Mexican position. Probably the Americans, who also referred to the fact that the Mexican constitution had been frequently amended, thought at the beginning that Mexico would modify its stand. Occasionally they were at odds in understanding Mexican positions and probably thought we were waiting—keeping oil as a negotiation chip—to get substantive concessions from the United States because in their opinion the opening of the energy sector would be beneficial to Mexico. The oil problem stayed alive on the U.S. side up to the very end. At a meeting in San Diego, ostensibly to watch a baseball game, President Bush once again—and for the last time—engaged President Salinas on the issue, only to be discreetly advised by Ambassador to Mexico John Negroponte that the subject was off limits.

Given the multiple initial restrictions and the occasionally acrimonious debate, it was a great feat to have arrived at a balanced approach where the United States and Canada did not insist on certain initial positions and Mexico found a way to accommodate concerns arising also from other sectors. Although oil exploration is still the preserve of the Mexican state, a door is opened to the sale of exploration services by foreign companies on a nonrisk sharing but special performance bonus basis. The petrochemical sector, also the preserve of the government, was redefined to include the eight most basic elements—ethane, propane, butane, pentane, hexane, eptane, and the naftas. For electricity, the construction and operation of private plants was allowed with the sale of the current made solely through the government-owned grid. Foreign companies may enter into supply agreements with Mexican entities under certain conditions. Pemex is subject to market restrictions and must manage market prices in its relations with clients. A minimum amount of government procurement has to be done through open international bidding—in the case of Pemex 50 percent is done immediately and 70 percent in seven years. It proved to be a great accomplishment and testimony to the skill of the negotiators to have settled this major obstacle in a rather elegant and fruitful way. The initial Mexican "no's" were sustained, which was crucial.

Problems abounded in many related sectors. Mexico wanted to raise its polypropylene tariff to its allowed GATT level while a new plant was planned, the United States being the main exporter to Mexico. The dyes and pigments sector was another political problem. Although most of the U.S. industry sustained a reduction in tariffs, the vast majority was foreign-owned, and one had to accommodate the one U.S.-owned corporation that had subsisted from old protectionist days and that wanted strict rules of origin. Something similar happened with the cosmetic/toiletry industry, which was pushing hard but had no real political clout against the presence of a major foreign competitor.

The powerful pharmaceutical industry was another matter. Probably 118 House members were identified as having substantial facilities in their districts or having received substantial PAC contributions for their campaigns. The issue here—intellectual property rights—was addressed through the new legislation that had recently been issued in Mexico. Americans wanted some further clarification of parallel imports—that is, the legal import into a country of medicines produced legitimately in foreign countries under a licensing agreement—and other issues and, as a tradeoff, were willing to accede to some protection of the local Mexican industry. It was certainly a protectionist attitude with minor liberal concessions.

Similarly, our Mexican team had to weigh the political cost of granting concessions in various sectors such as ceramics, where we would probably not encounter much congressional opposition to a fast staging of duty reductions for imports from Mexico. Chinaware should not cause much political concern if treated separately from glass, although some of the large producers raised great alarms. The value of glass imports from Mexico was at the time less than 1 percent of total U.S. imports.

Glass was a politically sensitive sector—a thorn to the very end. There are three main divisions in the industry: bottles and recipients, float glass, and glassware for the kitchen and dining room. This is a regionally determined industry. Bottles are mostly manufactured in Indiana, Pennsylvania, and West Virginia. Float glass, which is closely related to the auto and construction industries, comes mainly from Ohio and Michigan. Kitchen glassware is made in West Virginia, Arkansas, and Oklahoma. These geographically well-defined sectors exerted strong pressure, once again owing to the ability of regional groups to form congressional groups and caucuses. Moreover, because production processes vary quite a bit in the subsectors, it was difficult to achieve any sectoral balance through trade-offs. The United States particularly wanted to protect its kitchenware, but was pushing hard for a rapid opening of the Mexican market to U.S. float glass. Several corporations like Guardian were bearing their political weight against the supposed monopolist in Mexico—Vitro. The wildest exaggerations abounded. Vitro was said to be highly competitive, which is true, and a large corporation, which is true only if considered in the aggregate and not in each segment. Its capacity to produce the controversial float glass was but a fraction of the U.S. industry's. Yet Guardian, the U.S. corporation, could not appreciate the difference.

The Ohio and Michigan members who were pressuring for float glass included Marcy Kaptur, Howard Metzenbaum, John Glenn, and many others who were hard-core opponents and would not have been brought around even with concessions on this sector. Thus this made resistance that much easier. From the U.S. side, it was an exercise in rough, unsubtle tactics, although some good friends like Senators Richard Lugar, John Breaux, and Lloyd Bentsen had also been persuaded to pressure the Mexicans.

The home appliances industry provided an interesting example. Although initially located in the Midwest and Northeast, it had spread all over the United States, and several corporations involved had international ties. The industry is divided among five major manufacturers—Whirlpool, WCI, Maytag, Raytheon, and General Electric—and a number of smaller single-product producers. The first group, some of which had joint ventures in Mexico, tended to think globally and aimed at rationalizing their production facilities. They wanted a rapid staging out of tariffs both ways, whereas the smaller-niche-oriented U.S. firms, and the Mexicans as well, aimed at a slower pace without nevertheless blocking our way.

It required a great amount of skillful dedication to run after so many rabbits at the same time, trying to weigh divergent interests in terms of their political pressure without losing the overall concept of proceeding in a balanced, sustained manner toward free trade between two countries at totally different stages of economic development. The process was like forcing wild cats into a bag. As you search for cats still roaming around, you risked loosing some of the ones you thought you had already.

The negotiations of several sectors like the automotive industry and telecommunications were very difficult in another way. They provided rather the character of a protracted nuisance. Everybody was theoretically in agreement about the end result for both industries. But the protectionist legal structures in the three countries made it difficult to define the transition. Thus it was difficult for the other teams to fully grasp the sense and meaning of the Mexican Auto Decree and to find reasonable ways to transform it while at the same time allowing for its continuing operation.

In the United States, there were divergent views of the big three auto corporations—General Motors, Ford, and Chrysler—and the labor unions. The latter were concerned about job losses arising from companies moving to Mexico and about pressure from foreign competition to lower wages. The "big three" were interested in rationalizing the industry within the region, but were concerned about preventing Mexico from becoming a platform for non-NAFTA cars to be produced and exported to the United States. This ought to be negotiated within the context of the existing U.S.-Canada Auto-Pact, which had resulted in the near integration of the North American automotive industry, and the Mexican Auto Decree, requiring substantial domestic content for Mexican-made cars and the application of current CAFE (Energy Policy and Conservation Act of 1975) classifications to Mexican-made cars.

The Mexican Auto Decree, a convoluted concept that was difficult to understand and even more difficult to explain, required endless hours of study by the different groups looking into it. On one occasion Dr. Blanco used a series of equations to define the concepts involved. Jules Katz, his U.S. counterpart as chief negotiator, half in humor and half in desperation, said: "Listen Herminio, you get an A in algebra but an F in economics!"

The problems arising in the auto agreement had to be also considered in conjunction with CAFE, the U.S. system requiring minimum efficiencies for vehicles sold in the United States. Not every "regional" car could be considered "national" in the United States. Every U.S. corporation has to achieve a certain average efficiency in its domestic fleet. Therefore, as a probably undesirable effect, firms tended to manufacture abroad a good many luxury-car parts that were then not considered "domestic," thereby not pulling down average efficiency.

Existing structures had to be adjusted and transformed. In a way it was like modifying a building's structure while still using the building—a feat of architectural and engineering ingenuity. The tariff differentials—20 percent for foreign cars entering Mexico compared with 9.5 percent for Canada and 2.5 percent for the United States, had to be phased out while allowing for the protective features of the Auto Decree to be transformed in the process. Tariffs were immediately reduced to 10 percent, 4.6 percent, and 0 percent respectively for regional imports into Mexico, Canada, and the United States. Transitional quotas were imposed for different types of vehicles—cars, light trucks, and heavy duty trucks, and in the case of Mexico, different, stricter quotas were imposed for used vehicles. The rules of origin were set at a high 75 percent for regional value-added. Restrictions were eliminated to foreign capital participation in Mexico and a transformation of the system allowing certain local value-added requirements, providing for transitory import/export ratios.

In the telecommunications sector, negotiations were complicated. In Mexico, the recently privatized telephone company Telmex enjoyed, until 1997, a long-distance monopoly, and all three countries have some restrictions on foreign participation in radio and TV broadcasting. In these cases, the negotiations resembled the process of piecing together a puzzle with a theoretically clear but in its details blurred image of what the end result should be. How can the confusing variety of pieces that do not fit together be cut to the appropriate dimensions without losing the very meaning of those parts? This question applied especially to the technically and economically complex sectoral issues.

Another issue of contention was transportation. The United States is unabashedly protective of its maritime transportation industry. It was very difficult for us to understand that a small U.S. industry with fewer than 500 ships and 14,000 sailors would exert such political pressure to become the most protected industry. The economies of ocean shipping had overpriced U.S. ships, given high wage rates, large crew requirements, and high ship construction costs. In response to their declining economies, the maritime industry turned to the Congress for protection in the "Jones Act."

We had wanted to negotiate to have regional vessels be allowed for regional coastal trade. The U.S. answer was immediate and harsh: this was a deal-breaker; no further discussions allowed. The underlying rationale was based on economics, but rang totally like a "sovereignty" issue similar to the Mexican considerations about oil. Every nation, it was argued, must have sufficient maritime service to trade effectively and to provide emergency needs during wartime. Among other antique practices, unions in the maritime industry actually pay their members—in cash in large bills—at the port of disembarkation. The paymaster is also the collector for the PAC, and it is easy for him to solicit large donations from members, thereby tightening the interest of assorted members of Congress. The shipowners are equally generous. Because this industry works Congress so diligently, not surprisingly every bill that provides for shipments of any federally financed cargo is amended to provide for a cargo preference for U.S. flag vessels.

Maritime transportation provided a unique case, but protectionist pressure was rampant in the whole transportation sector. The Mexican trucking sector flew into a state of panic, fearing U.S. competition and its enormous financial resources. The U.S. unions bolstered the fears of truck drivers that they would be swamped by low-earning Mexicans not subject to the same restrictions applying in the United States. In fact all drivers—and trucks—are subject to the same norms in each of the countries involved, and claims to the contrary were dishonest but powerful. Thus in cases like this the contentious problems were of little technical complexity but mired in politics and disingenuous fearmongering.

The overall result was quite balanced. Because of the nature of this sector, it was agreed that revisions would take place in the fifth year and afterward at two-year intervals. Comparable norms would be used for transportation equipment and transborder service, which is initially allowed in the border states and is later applied to the rest of the countries exclusively for international cargo.

The financial sector had special significance, given its nature and role in the overall negotiating process. Mexico's financial sector forbade foreign participation, with a minor exception that illuminates Mexican political culture. During the bloody days of the Mexican Civil War—in Spanish "La Revolucion"—after 1910, the country almost disintegrated into rival factions and regions. In the chaos, nearly all the foreign banks left the country. Citibank nevertheless stayed, and to acknowledge its loyal attitude toward the country, Mexico allowed it to be the one foreign financial institution that could operate.

The United States was particularly interested in the opening of this sector, which we knew was necessary to bolster the competitiveness of Mexico's domestic sector and to attract foreign capital. Apart from several difficult issues, like the national control of each country's payments system and the handling of foreign exchange policy, the problem was timing. Here the Mexicans could play a chip of great relevance to the United States. If played with skill, it could win a maximum of concessions in other parts of the negotiations without openly linking them. The skill with which this was handled reflects the professional and political acumen of the negotiators. Initially the assumption was made that the financial services sector was of paramount importance for Americans and could be used for trade-offs in another sector. This assumption proved to be invalid. U.S. commercial banks, the sector with more political influence, was at the time totally taken up by pressures for domestic reform deriving from a revision of specialized banking. Investment banks and brokerage firms, which would be more interested, lacked the political clout to provide Mexico with adequate trade-offs for its own concessions in financial services. Nevertheless, although it did achieve a balance of specific concessions, it proved to be an asset of generalized value that was several times used rather skillfully by Dr. Serra in the final days of the negotiations.

In Congress, we faced strong opposition in the committees of jurisdiction, headed by Representative Henry Gonzalez, chairman of the House Banking Committee, Representative John Dingell of Energy and Commerce, and Senator Donald Riegle, chairman of the Banking, Housing, and Urban Affairs Committee.

In principle, all countries opened their financial systems to the others. Our discussions of balance in the agreement referred to the quite notable difference between the U.S. and the Mexican financial sectors: even a total opening of each country does not have for the other an equivalent value. This was an issue that could not be solved. The Mexican sector allows universal banking with all financial services provided under one roof and is federal in nature without state restrictions. Nonetheless, the U.S. system was already open to foreigners, which for Mexico did not count for much; given its scarce resources, Mexico could not take advantage of all the opportunities involved.

Finally, the Mexican financial sector opened different categories with transitory limits for foreign market participation until the year 2000. During that period, each foreign regional commercial bank cannot have more than 1.5 percent of the sectoral assets, and the accumulated foreign investment cannot surpass 15 percent of total. Similar schedules were set for brokerage firms, insurance companies, nonbank banks (for example, American Express and GM Finance Corporation), etc.

Foreign investment is one of the sectors of greatest relevance and in principle the least contentious, because, as in the financial sector, Mexican and U.S. positions were not that far apart. Obviously Mexico was starting from a rather restrictive environment and tradition, and the problem was more about domestic negotiations with different sectors that felt threatened by foreign investment. The final outcome allowed national treatment to foreign investment, and, with some exceptions that were taken by each country (which appear in an annex and pertain mostly to energy, petrochemicals, transportation), the scope of the opening was rather wide. The single most debated issue, and certainly highly significant in Mexican legal tradition, is the one related to the so-called Calvo clause, a principle of Mexican international policy that does not allow any foreign company operating in Mexico to sue the Mexican government. This clause has historical meaning based on the experience of foreign navies' (French, English, and Spanish) taking over Mexican ports to impose the presumed rights of their national companies (referred to in Mexican history as "Guerra de los Pasteles" or "Pastry War," because some French bakeries were involved). This also was solved in a difficult and elegant way.

Probably the most contentious issues, from the U.S. stand-point, were related to dispute settlement. In this field, Canadian and Mexican interests converged in principle. The controversy—which spread through the whole of the negotiations—was really the last important issue. Take the U.S. handling of foreign commerce. The United States has had an ample tradition of promoting free international trade, but only insofar as it does not affect specific interests. To reconcile these opposing views, the U.S. system opens trade but keeps it simultaneously under threat of unilateral sanctions. A number of laws provide the U.S. business sector with trade remedies against perceived unjust foreign competition, whether through government subsidies, dumping at prices lower than domestic ones, foreign violations of commercial agreements, or simply foreign practices that are deemed discriminatory and restrictive to commerce originating in the United States. From a foreign point of view, the United States in practice allows itself to interpret agreements rather broadly in its own interest without accepting the decisions of international tribunals or even subjecting itself to them. It also gives itself ample leeway to regard foreign commercial policies as imposing undue barriers and permits, or practically requires, U.S. retaliation. These are principles of so-called fair trade, and during the negotiations we had to consider that their most notable proponent in Congress was Majority Leader Richard Gephardt, who played a crucial, negative role in the ratification of NAFTA.

These problems had been of paramount importance during the negotiations of the Canada-U.S. free trade agreement and became a deal-breaker. The agreement itself was salvaged at the last moment by a U.S. concession for a temporary mechanism to solve disputes through the appointment of panels. During the NAFTA negotiations these concerns arose from the start, and it was of the utmost importance to Mexico, as the economically weaker party, that a balanced, objective system be established to solve trade disputes within the agreement. Every time this subject came up during the negotiations, Jules Katz turned red and with contained rage simply stated this matter was out of bounds for discussion. Nevertheless, its importance to us was such that we continuously brought it back. The Americans were finally ready to make great concessions to obtain the agreement when they relented in their opposition and were disposed to discuss it.

Both chapters XIX and XX thus emerged—the first on remedies to disloyal commercial practices such as subsidies and dumping, and the second on controversies arising from measures taken by a country that are deemed to be incompatible with the agreement or that cause a reduction or annulment of the benefits established in it. The initial Mexican position toward antidumping procedures was that they are meaningless and irrational once a common market is operating in the absence of tariffs. Theoretically the existence of one market would make dumping internationally as impossible as it is domestically. Clearly, once tariffs are eliminated between two countries, prices would tend to become the same because any difference would trigger signals to import from the low-priced country. Any dumping in another country would be impossible as a permanent practice; price differences would be rather comparable to a "sale" in another region or the offering of special discounts within the same country. Only during the transition would dumping occur. In lieu of antidumping, one would rather have to consider adopting antitrust regulations. But the Americans insisted on having this weapon in their arsenal even if theoretically it were not at all needed.

Perhaps the finest example of how the agreement developed into a widely encompassing concept based on a decision by all parties to be cooperative and understanding was the solution given to this most delicate of subjects. The first element involved minimizing problems that would develop into disputes through the whole system of supervision by the Free Trade Commission and the Secretariat with its three national sections and a number of committees and working groups. Further, if a controversy were to arise, it would first trigger consultations among the parties that, if unsuccessful, would lead to conciliation and mediation. If the problems are not resolved, a dispute settlement panel is called on to intervene. The manner in which a panel would be convened and its members appointed is a great testimony to the spirit that finally prevailed in the whole agreement—one of almost exquisite fairness. A roster of 30 panelists is formed from the list of 10 names submitted by each country, and each country can initially veto the inclusion of certain individuals. If a dispute arises between two countries, a 5-member panel is chosen in a peculiar cross-choice manner. Each country chooses 2 panelists out of the list proposed by the other country. The presiding panelist is chosen by mutual agreement, and should this fail, a drawing would be taken to determine which party would have the right to name this individual; in any case the person cannot be a national of the choosing party. This system of cross-choice, conceived by the Mexican delegation, is really the crown-jewel of fairness. It compresses the sense of the whole agreement and epitomizes its spirit.

A similar system for panel appointments is used in antidumping cases, except that the panel has to pass judgment as to whether the sued country did appropriately follow its own rules. An international panel, not an international authority, thus judges each country's laws and regulations. This system reflects the care taken to respect each country's legal system, national sensitivities, and idiosyncracies while providing simultaneously for a fair and unbiased dispute-settlement process.

From a foreign point of view, the United States enters trade agreements only when it retains the ability to carry a big stick if conditions run against its interests. Although no one had the power to take away the stick, it was at least possible to limit its arbitrary use. The Americans had conceded a similar, though not as elaborate, system in the Canadian trade agreement as a last-minute effort to salvage it, but it was considered temporary. NAFTA makes it permanent and contains a proof of fairness by the way panelists are chosen.

The problem of timing was continuously important to the whole process. Each country had a different political and legislative timing that were extremely difficult to synchronize. The fast track imposed rigidities within which negotiations had to take place and strict stages for signature and consideration by the Congress. From the start we always thought and planned for windows of opportunity or times when the political skies gave the right opening. We prepared several games regarding diverse political and legislative scenarios that gave the right configuration of stars. As a matter of fact the whole process was enacted within a window of opportunity that arose with the elections of Presidents Salinas and Bush. But we needed a specific opportunity to accelerate and finish the negotiations proper because the complexity of issues dragged them on and on. The right timing—politically— arrived at the end of spring and the beginning of summer 1992 with the imminent electoral campaign. We could sense an impetus to reach decisions and a proclivity to solve problems rather than to set up road-blocks on the way. President Bush needed a final agreement before the Republican and Democratic conventions. We could smell the end in the same way one can sense the ocean in a salty, open breeze.

This volume dwells almost exclusively on the U.S.-Mexican aspects of NAFTA because of the vantage point of the author. Canada very skillfully played a role that was at times low key to the point of evanescence and at times highly visible and dramatic. When Canada entered the negotiations on February 5, 1991, its defensive attitude seemed to say that it sensed little to gain. Its trade with Mexico was minute, and it already had an agreement with the United States. Nevertheless, Canada would lose if it were not part of the new agreement and if the Americans conceded to Mexico elements potentially detrimental to Canada. Canada's insistence on participating was thus viewed with mixed feelings by some in both delegations. Mexico did willingly accept Canada's inclusion because, apart from potential commercial advantages, politically it nullified arguments that Mexico would be subjecting itself ignominiously to the dictates of the United States. It also sent a message to Latin American countries that the free trade concept was multinational and thus open to access by other continental nations.

Initially Canada played a passive role because the main arguments were between the United States and Mexico. Occasionally during this stage the Canadian negotiators intervened as honest brokers and played the role of a buffer when discussions became tough. But at several crucial points and certainly at the end, Canada skillfully played the protagonist by waiting for an agreement to be at hand on a certain sector and then in effect taking it hostage until its own concerns were addressed. So repeatedly was this the case in different groups that the non-Canadian negotiators were ready to blow up in rage. In this way Canada finally emerged with different treatments in agriculture and textiles and also strove for a separate auto industry chapter. When exasperated at the stalling tactics regarding a point that had already been finalized to our satisfaction, we sometimes thought the best solution would be to finalize a U.S.-Mexico agreement and then let Canada adhere to it if it so wished.

The most dramatic moments occurred during the last ten days of negotiations. Although the negotiations had started on August 2 with shared hopes for a speedy finish, they lasted until August 12. Canada was caught in a dilemma because it had sold – with good reason – the revised chapters dealing with antidumping procedures revisions as a great victory during its own agreement with the United States. Now that this was extended to Mexico, the problem arose that the panel decisions may in practice be nugatory for Mexico because of the existence of the "amparo" law, whereby Mexican citizens are protected from acts of government. Things went very far when Canada suggested that Mexico as a newcomer to the free trade agreement have a separate deal on dispute resolutions in which Canada would have no part. This was unreasonable and offensive: it had been the United States and Mexico who had started the process and had accepted Canada's request to be part of it. Tempers finally subsided and an understanding was reached on the subject. At the end, Canada raised a problem related to the financial sector that nearly exasperated the other negotiators.

Each country obviously has to defend its own interests intelligently. In this sense Canada's participation in the negotiations was at times subdued and low key, but at other times harsh and unremitting when it really mattered. This was the right and intelligent way for them to go about defending their interests. The negotiations faced formidable obstacles because of the many differences – in levels of economic development, legal and cultural traditions, and historic animosities or prejudices. These differences were surmounted with great creativity and fairness, which pays tribute to the people most responsible for the negotiations in the three countries. After the *pas de deux* that characterized the initial stages, the national teams, with their varying interests and diverse points of view, appreciated their common mission and partnership. This splendid sign of cooperation between countries became abundantly clear when, in the wee hours of August 12, after the final handshake of the ministers, a wave of joy over-whelmed all participants. Champagne bottles were opened, and everybody embraced in the high spirits of shared victory.

3

The Political Stage and
Side Agreements

Since the beginning of the negotiations, environmental and labor issues were the main concern around which the opposition clustered. When we arrived in Washington to open a Mexican office to support the administration's getting the fast-track authorization, the trade unions and NGOs had already taken over the battlefield. They had preempted any effort from our side and were certainly on top of things.

Opponents were connected for the most part with that disorganized entity known, according to Will Rogers the famous Oklahoman, as the Democratic Party. Assorted groups ranging from the trade unions, church-affiliated and urban ethnic associations, Blacks and Hispanics, southern conservatives, and greens, were in one way or another related to the Democrats, who were as a partisan matter opposed to the agreement if for no other reason than because it was a concept proposed by the Mexicans but accepted by the governing Republican Party.

The very nature of a free trade agreement provoked negative reactions of various sorts. It would be entered into with a poor neighboring country with which inciting prejudice was easy and carrying out an enlightened argument difficult, given different cultures and traditional values. Objectivity would be hard to achieve.

Initially the Mexican reaction was to resist the pressure for

73

considering environmental and labor issues without appreciating their political strength and the underlying global trend toward linking them with trade. Finally accommodation was sought, and the agreement itself took account of environmental issues in such a way that it became the "greenest" of trade agreements negotiated. Thus we and the Bush administration thought we had adequately addressed the issues—but it was not to be.

As discussed earlier, President Bush had responded with an "Action Plan" to letters from Senator Bentsen and Congressman Rostenkowski on these issues. Majority Leader Gephardt with Rostenkowski's support had produced H.R. 146, which had been voted on the same day as the fast-track measure. It seemed to us that both the contents of the agreement making it the "greenest" ever and acts of the president had adequately addressed those concerns. The text of the agreement contains novel environmental provisions that commit the signatories to pursue policies of sustainable development, permit each country to impose nondiscriminatory and higher health, safety, and environmental standards, bar the waiver of environmental regulations as an incentive for investment, ensure that specified environmental agreements will take precedence over NAFTA, and place the burden on the complainant in dispute settlement procedures to prove that an environmental standard is a disguised barrier to trade.

In January 1992, the president went further and announced a comprehensive and streamlined federal job training system. Building on it, on August 14, 1992, the president proposed a new $10 billion worker adjustment initiative covering all dislocated workers and offering temporary assistance helping them find more secure jobs, training assistance in the form of skill grants, and transition income support when necessary for workers completing retraining. Any nonpartisan assessment would have considered realistic concerns satisfied. But opinions on social issues tend to polarize, especially when argued in the context of a harsh presidential election debate.

The efforts to integrate labor and environmental considerations into a free trade agreement between countries at different stages of economic development arose from different, and on occasion disparate, sources:

• deep-felt concern about labor and human rights and protection of natural resources ran the spectrum from moderation to what we might call economic primitivism—that is, a failure to consider the economic restrictions or a "go back to the caves" attitude;

• protectionist attitudes that regard existing disparities in those sectors as undue comparative advantages;

• big-brother reactions that consider—without obviously admitting it in the open—that some countries because of their higher development status or power have a moral right to impose their notions on other peoples.

It is certainly very difficult to sort out the legitimate concerns from those that simply mask other purposes, and to distinguish reasonable from purely emotional arguments. This entanglement of motivations and discourse made labor and the environment politically flammable issues, which was the last thing Mexicans wanted.

The Campaign and NAFTA

The more moderate Democrats had come out at times with provisos in favor of the agreement. Conspicuous among them was Governor Bill Clinton, who in the Michigan primaries clearly supported it. Clinton appeared the winner in the political process although somewhat weak, with Paul Tsongas on the one side, appealing to moderate middle-class Democrats, and Jerry Brown on the other, acting like a political rebel and providing shelter for those in search of a cause.

The issue of NAFTA was ominously raised in a Pennsylvania senatorial campaign—the by-election of college-president-turned-candidate Harris Wofford for the seat of John Heinz, who had died in a plane accident. Wofford's two main campaign issues were health care, which badly needed reform and later became a central issue for candidate (and later president) Clinton, and NAFTA, which he opposed. If his opposition got extensive popular support, it would spread and be taken as a central campaign issue by other politicians. This was the last thing we wanted. Some newspapers like the *Philadelphia Inquirer*, while supporting Wofford, took exception to his stand on NAFTA. Luckily NAFTA did not arouse much interest, and we were somewhat relieved. The manager of the successful campaign was James Carville, who made a name for himself there and later went to work for Clinton during his presidential campaign and subsequently at the White House. This forebode ill for the proponents of NAFTA, but later the same person became, as we shall see, very influential in searching for a moderate position just before the final vote on NAFTA in 1993.

This fragile political situation was not helped by President Bush's decision to raise NAFTA as a campaign issue. For the Mexican side, it was the wrong tactic because several opinion polls, including one made for us, revealed either a high level of ignorance or an important core of opposition. President Bush chose nevertheless to challenge Clinton on the issue and, because Clinton was subject to many opposing groups in the Democratic Party, which made strong decisions in this area difficult, to portray him as a waverer who could not make up his mind.

As far as we were concerned, we were entering a minefield, given the recent history of the official Democratic Party's position. In March 1991, before the fast-track vote, its platform had been clearly critical and opposed to the NAFTA proposal. That was a very serious warning for the new platform in the electoral cycle of 1992. Although there was little we could do directly, we had friends who were aware of the potential problem and could do something about it. And they did. When Bill Richardson became the secretary to the platform drafting committee, the most radical language was disposed of, softening somewhat the official stand of the Democrats. Still the situation was rather fragile.

In these unsettling circumstances, the Mexican tradition of dealing internationally and officially only with parties in government made it difficult to reach out directly to the Democrats and try to influence the moderates in their approach to NAFTA. Our team members debated among themselves and finally, in consultations with President Salinas himself, gave approval for me to start contacting the Democrats in the campaign. Barry Carter, a Georgetown law professor, was appointed the contact man for the party.

Our relations were simple. I explained to him the general trends of the discussions and detailed the baseless objections of our opponents. We were approaching the end of negotiations, and through Democrats in government, Clinton's campaign people had all the information they wanted. For our part, it was more a problem of political courtesy than anything else. On their side they conveyed their dissatisfaction, for example, with the proposed meeting of Presidents Salinas and Bush in San Diego that would occur during a baseball match and be given a low profile. We were concerned lest candidate Clinton succumb to the pressure of the many opponents that swarmed the party and geared much of our effort to preparing papers discussing NAFTA. We learned that some of them were used as a basis for discussions with the candidate himself. We were very much relieved to hear that they were looking for a way to approve of NAFTA in principle while subjecting it to certain conditions that at the time we thought would be cosmetic.

Word had circulated in Mexico that the government had at great risk put all its eggs in Bush's basket and that this had complicated our relations with the Democrats, but it was not so. It is true that our relations with the Bush administration were excellent and our opposition was centered in the Democratic Party, but we cultivated friendships in both parties. We foresaw the change in administration and were prepared to bridge that gap effectively and appropriately.

The final position on NAFTA came in October 1992. At a speech in North Carolina, Clinton approved the concept, arguing that it was a typically flawed Bush deal that needed to be bolstered by special agreements on labor, the environment, and safeguards. Safeguards had been adequately treated in NAFTA apart from its openness to the GATT's procedures on the subject. So I went to the Democrats' Washington headquarters to state that this element had quite properly been addressed. Although the charge was not formally dropped, at later stages it was finessed to mean that we needed statistical early warning systems to prevent the occurrence. Nevertheless, for some time, probably owing to inadequate information within the party during his confirmation hearings, Mickey Kantor, the newly appointed U.S. Trade Representative, forcefully returned to this issue. At these hearings Kantor emphasized that safeguards had to be reinforced without opening the agreement itself—a contradiction in terms.

The contacts with the Democrats were raised to a higher level. José Córdoba took over from me and had a first meeting with Barry Carter and Anthony Lake that produced a sensation in Mexico. It became the subject of a Mexican newspaper article that included purported details of the meeting—actual information about the discussion, what each person ordered, and who paid the bill. We knew the Mexican side had not leaked it—only three or four people knew about it on our side. We were sure it was the Americans, but we failed to understand their purpose. They vehemently denied involvement, and we eventually learned that reporters had managed to introduce high sensitivity listening gear into the restaurant.

The New Team

Governor Clinton's election victory made it paramount for Mexico to enter into direct contact with him. The very next day after the election, Mexican ambassador Gustavo Petricioli went to Little Rock and extended probably the first congratulations of any chief of state. We were highly interested in having President Salinas meet with President-elect Clinton, but first we had to cross a hurdle that could spell problems with the new administration but was required to keep up NAFTA's momentum. President Bush wanted to be the person to sign the agreement because he had been the one who had negotiated and fought for it consistently and clearly. The Democrats would have willed it differently: they would not accept "Bush's" agreement, but had to show due deference to the presidential office they just had won and therefore accept Bush's agreement. It was duly signed in San Antonio in December 1992. Care was taken nevertheless to avoid making it an overly ceremonious affair.

It was thus imperative that the Clinton and Salinas meeting take place even before the inauguration. We placed a great deal of emphasis on this because, although we knew that Clinton conditionally favored the agreement, we cared that he give a sign to the Democratic Party and the country as a whole about its importance. Finally a meeting was arranged through the good offices of Governor Ann Richards of Texas at her executive mansion in Austin. It got off to a good start; Salinas and Clinton chatted for close to an hour and a half with no witnesses present and afterward came down the stairways smiling, their mood relaxed and friendly. One of the members of the Mexican commission was Luis Donaldo Colosio, who spoke at length with Al Gore whom he had met at a world environmental conference in Rio de Janeiro. They shared a common interest in environmental matters and got along very well. Colosio would later become presidential candidate in Mexico and be tragically assassinated in Tijuana in March 1994.

The preinauguration period brought a mixture of hopes and uncertainties. Uncertainties finally prevailed, however, because it was never clear when the campaign had ended and a real government program had begun. Any government program needs a clear setting of priorities and adequate staffing at the right time. In several of these aspects the new administration proved lacking. Although intellectual jamborees like the Renaissance Meeting in Little Rock inspired a host of ideas, the new administration did not advance a coherent plan. Defending gays in the military, reneging on the Haitian refugee pledge, and dealing with the attorney general designate's problem in omitting Social Security payments for her Peruvian nanny and driver were all self-inflicted wounds that betrayed a group fertile in ideas and plentiful in energy but unable to deliver a government program in line with the campaign's middle-of-the-road pledges.

The problem arose from the innate contradiction of the early Clinton presidency. The president wanted dearly to be true to his campaign promises, especially the ones on tax relief for the middle class and reform of the health care system. He also wanted to spur the economy through an investment program in order to get credit for any economic growth, which was actually already beginning. Instead he saw himself forced to give priority to deficit reduction, which precluded some of his cherished items but would give the bond market a push in the right direction, lowering long-term interest rates and thereby stimulating investment. But this was scarcely a democratic government program. The health care issue in particular was dealt severe blows even at this stage well before it was put to rest by design complications and the increased government intervention it entailed.

This political schizophrenia contained an underlying conflict between a mostly young entourage of campaign-fresh tacticians and the Washington-wise, Wall-Street-involved "old boys" – two groups that pulled in opposing directions. The president's heart was probably with the former, his mind with the latter. Anyway, these circumstances generated little interest and attention for NAFTA, which was considered by the mainstream in the president's party as little more than an annoyance.

These problems obviously affected the way NAFTA issues were addressed. For several months there was a vacuum, while recently appointed government officials were apparently at a loss of how to address these issues. And since nature abhors a vacuum, and politicians even more, we, the Mexican team, feared that an opening was being given to the most radical opponents who could take the agreement hostage and either set impossible conditions or suffocate it through delay.

For several weeks after the inauguration we heard very little from the Americans. Because the proposal for the side agreements had originated with them, we believed we should wait and see what they were up to and simply prepare for different scenarios, from the most radical to the more moderate. We were simply disconcerted, however, and finally agreed that we should have our own point of view clearly defined and ready to propose if we saw an undefined or wavering position on the other side.

At his confirmation hearings, Mickey Kantor had made vigorous statements about strict labor and environmental conditions for NAFTA, but we thought the final U.S. position would be softer because any other course would not be in the interests of the United States. On the one hand, we supposed the Americans knew that the Mexican, and Canadian, reaction to a harsh proposal would be uncompromisingly negative. On the other hand, we understood that the United States could not propose strong mandates for Occupational Safety and Health Administration–type norms or strike procedures. Mexico could answer with the demand that Mexican labor regulations such as no-striker replacement, three-month maternity leave, or lay-off compensations be also obligatory for U.S. workers, which would have been a fair tit-for-tat if positions became too radical. These would never be accepted by the Americans and so neither could we accept their regulations simply because they thought them to be fair. These regulations also provide an example of a Mexican labor law that is quite strictly enforced and goes beyond the concepts of Democratic liberals.

On the environmental side, we also thought the Americans would not risk harassing Mexican companies lest American companies themselves be harassed. The Americans have always been extremely sensitive about accepting anything that could be construed as a supra-national authority. We were sure that any imposition on their part that would legally and logically open the way to having Canada and Mexico do likewise would not be contemplated. Thus, we thought, there was a built-in set of restrictions about what the Americans would propose that would obviate the need to face the most extreme positions.

But we were proven wrong. Probably a lack of governing experience and the exhilaration of victory energized our American counterpart, as well as simple political greed—a version of greed as a U.S. impulse articulated by the future President Truman in 1937. It was the result of a supremacist attitude under the guise of moralistic principles that has not been absent in U.S. foreign policy. We had miscalculated the new administration when its proposal was finally presented in Ottawa in April 1993.

Difficult Times

The road to April was filled with skirmishes that were the new administration's tactical effort to conceal a lack of a thorough, logical position. NAFTA was certainly not one of their priorities, and to our regret they would need time to establish a negotiating position. As February passed, the new administration was fighting detrimental, unfocused side-battles like subsidies to the European Airbus and threats of getting out of GATT on government procurement issues. Its most important policies concentrated not on NAFTA but on the health care system, the budget, and training and education. The latter was certainly connected to NAFTA but otherwise not much movement was perceived in issues of our direct concern.

The Mexican team became nervous because of the delay in the further negotiations for NAFTA. We were facing a serious political problem if the agreement were not finished and ratified by the end of 1993. The Mexican presidential campaign traditionally would begin then. To delay the approval of NAFTA would seriously jeopardize the whole electoral debate in Mexico, given that the president had invested so much political capital in it and that anti-NAFTA forces were certainly present within several groups of the governing party itself and in the opposition from the left. Several of us believed that if no progress were evident during the first three months of the new administration, it would be in Mexico's best interest to discontinue the negotiations. President Salinas seemed to hold a similar view in an interview with the *Washington Post* on February 22, 1993.

A preview of the bumpy road ahead came the first time Mexican Secretary Serra met in Washington with U.S. Trade Representative Kantor. His visit occasioned an act of political terrorism by Majority Leader Gephardt, no friend of the negotiations, when he claimed in a letter to the president of Mexico that Alfonso Peniche, a businessman from Yucatan, with the help of his government was engaged in a program of buying labor-intensive U.S. firms and resetting them to Mexico. Although this was a gross misstatement because the program aimed at companies that were failing in the States, it provided a convenient political target. Kantor used this issue in a singularly abrupt, intelligent way but certainly not in a manner conducive to any smooth handling of the negotiations about to begin. He tried with aplomb to set Secretary Serra off-balance. Those were the political instincts of a street-wise fighter giving little consideration to issues and much to gaining tactical political advantage. No wonder he had been the presidential campaign manager for President Clinton. In particular, the issue was that a Mexican government development bank, Nafin, was behind the scheme. Secretary Serra explained that any participation of Nafin in the affair was only temporary according to its own policies. Anyway, the way the program was structured simply reflected creative entrepreneurial attitude and did not harm anybody, least of all the bankrupt U.S. companies that were the targets. Nevertheless its slogan, "Yes you can, Yucatan," became a battle cry for the opposition to the agreement first in the hands of Gephardt and then as a useful tool for the likes of Ross Perot, a not insignificant latecomer to the NAFTA debate.

Gephardt had played a significant role during the fast-track procedures but somehow his extreme impulses, fueled by his assistant Michael Wessel, were at that time restrained by the intervention of Ways and Means chairman Rostenkowski. But at this stage he went out of bounds, first by willfully misinterpreting the Yucatan program and by writing the Mexican president. He then publicly disclosed his letter, which lacked a minimal degree of respect. His timing was shrewd: the union leaders had their annual Florida meeting during those days, and by attracting their and the government's attention he gained leverage to influence later stages of this process. He subsequently traveled several times to the Mexican border on one-day "fact-finding" missions where the only discovery made is the one being sought. In several speeches, he later described a Mexican worker, one Mr. Mendez, who was asking Gephardt for help with the inhuman conditions of his job, obviously implying general criticism of the Mexican system and setting up the majority leader as savior. That was certainly a new calling for Dick Gephardt. He tried to become the sanctimonious anti-Bush, anti-NAFTA hero and insisted on visiting the Mexican president and having a joint press conference. The meeting was finally granted but without the media exposure, which was blatant conceit. The fact that he had even thought such a démarche possible betrayed his lack of perception for another country's feelings and etiquette.

Not every development was negative. We knew that candidate Clinton had made a courageous and statesmanlike decision against the recommendations of some of his political advisers by accepting NAFTA, albeit conditionally. He returned as president to insist, in a speech at American University on February 26, that open markets would generate exports and employment at higher wages. NAFTA was mentioned in the second of his five points. Even Gephardt, rallying the opposition forces while speaking at an International Affairs Committee hearing about his being against the "Bush-NAFTA" agreement, answered a question raised by Representative Torricelli that yes, he was for NAFTA in principle.

The side agreement negotiations started with a meeting in Arlington, Virginia, with very general statements from the United States that were open to interpretation, depending upon future developments. In mid-April discussions continued at the Camino Real Hotel in Mexico City, where Canada proposed a particularly logical approach to labor and environmental issues strictly within the context of trade. The American position was obviously not completely spelled out and included what to some of us seemed like incongruities.

Mexico did not propose any document at that time. Mexican negotiators had been strengthened by the collaboration of high officials of both the Secretaría de Desarrollo Social or Sedesol (integrating the environmental department) and the Labor Ministry. Santiago Oñate of Sedesol was a sharp and witty participant—a resourceful and creative but also down-to-earth colleague whose sparkling conversation I greatly enjoyed. Norma Samaniego, undersecretary of labor, possessed a subtle, intelligent touch that enabled her to sail across rough subjects—and people— unscathed without losing toughness.

The problems to consider could be analyzed, I thought, within a framework that included first the scope. It could be very ample, including any labor law and environmental issue, or could be restricted to a particular set. The second point would be the standing of different persons or institutions to raise problems at the several institutions that would be established to deal with them. The third point of contention would be the precise nature of those institutions and the type of sanctions that would be permitted. Fourth, financial aspects had to be considered as in any program, especially if they had to do with border issues. Fifth, the all-encompassing problem was to connect the diverse issues with trade: after all, we were facing agreements supplementary to a free trade agreement!

All the issues were highly flammable. Many groupings had their say, from the environmentalists of the Sierra Club and militant church groups to Jesse Jackson's Rainbow Coalition, which promised demonstrations at the border or at any plant that would be closing because of NAFTA. Corporate America on the other hand was sitting on its hands, fearing that Mexico would concede too much to radical positions to finalize the agreement. Mexico had no intention of doing so, but neither was it on a merely cosmetic expedition. Some of the issues raised were serious, and the task was to separate and eradicate the weed that was intertwined with the good herb. Some groups initiated interesting efforts that suggested a middle ground—for example, a speech by Senator Max Baucus, an influential environmentalist, before the American Bar Association, which provided a basis for fruitful negotiations.

The administration was caught between its rhetoric and its desire to accommodate. There was continuous reference to an agreement with "teeth"—that is, the use of hard sanctions to impose labor and environmental regulations on nations at fault. These remarks were directed to Mexico, but nevertheless in the way they were stated the administration risked biting its own lips. Whatever means the United States was free to use against other countries within the agreements could be used against the United States itself, and the U.S. record was not as clean as was pretended. Too much puritan rhetoric about sanctions concealed the main problem and only risked sinking the agreements. This was probably the underlying purpose of many but it had been taken over by misguided people of good will.

The way to go about it was more practical: define the problem; search for doable solutions; visualize the resources needed. Our position was straightforward: in the spirit of cooperation to devise the best ways to have NAFTA clearly become a means to improve the environment and the enforcement of labor rights.

Politically we thought a reasonable agreement would be not only effective but saleable. In the U.S. Congress, a bipartisan coalition had to be formed if there were any serious intention to pass NAFTA, and we were sure it would make a satisfactory majority. We followed trends as closely as possible and thought we could count on 120 Republicans and 70 Democrats in Congress to favor a NAFTA with moderate side agreements. President Clinton would be able to deliver 30 more Democrats, and we would assure passage.

The first time I gave these estimates to a ranking Democrat dealing with the negotiations, he stopped me and said sarcastically: "Hermann, when did you get that enlightenment? You don't understand that this has to be not a Republican but a Democratic victory. It has to be Clinton's agreement." I was certainly confused and retorted they would never get the agreement passed even if, *dato et non concesso*, the Mexicans and Canadians were to accept a drift to the left in the side agreements. They would be losing two Republicans for every one Democrat the more they departed from the moderate mainstream to please the related trade union and other liberals. To me that answer was ominous and forebode bad tidings. We were facing people with scant understanding of the issues and little sense of what was politically feasible even in their own backyard—unless it was simply a charade to torpedo the whole process, which, in deference to their intelligence, it probably was. This continued to be our argument, and we were encouraged by our estimates of congressional members with environmental concerns moderate enough to be brought over by reasonable agreements. By our estimates, we could count on House endorsements from 33 Democrats and 7 Republicans. We also thought we could get the backing of moderate environmental associations like the World Wildlife Fund, although never the Friends of the Earth and the Sierra

Club. And it was a bad omen that little encouragement came from important individuals in the administration.

The problem was that the Democrats were still riding on a recent democratic victory, and, despite the president's lead, some of the politicos surrounding him never favored NAFTA. They thought it was politically a no-win issue and would have rather strangled it to free the president for other items in his and their agenda. Nevertheless, NAFTA was part of the president's agenda, and he badly needed a political victory of the sort NAFTA could give him if treated in a reasonable way and not stretched to accommodate Gephardt and his leftist cohorts. Several people at the White House were also radically oriented; one of them, Howard Paster, even accused us Mexicans of playing the Republican game against the Democrats. At later stages he nuanced his position and was finally helpful in pushing for NAFTA passage.

The real crisis that had been looming erupted during the negotiations held in Ottawa on May 19 through 21. In an ample room overlooking the magnificent houses of Parliament across the Ottawa River, the Americans proposed their long overdue positions, which were disturbingly worse than we had expected. They may be called *Kafkaesque* or surrealistic or simply unrealistic. They proposed to address a very wide scope of issues and gave very broad standing to the public, who could raise issues that in the end could, after a restrictive filtering process, result in trade sanctions. The initial opening was so large that it could subject our government to continuous harassment. The last thing the Mexicans wanted was to become a society subject to a flow of litigation from north of the border.

The Canadians and Mexicans reacted predictably with a simple no. On those bases, negotiations could not proceed. As the meetings drew to a close, the usual press conference was scheduled, and the problem was how to deal publicly with the embarrassing situation created. U.S. chief negotiator Rufus Yerxa proposed that divergences be stated as they had occurred—a risky strategy that could unleash a process difficult to control in each one of our countries. We wondered what the underlying intentions were. Quite divergent interpretations were possible: one was to establish the opposition in Canada and Mexico so clearly that a message could be sent to the White House about the lack of feasibility of such an approach; another was to rally liberal groups to force the other countries to torpedo the agreement. We leaned toward the first interpretation and were probably right. This was risky, however, because at the time both houses in Congress were considering the reconciliation law for the president's deficit reduction package. The law finally passed under strictly partisan votes with all Republicans against. This was not a good omen for NAFTA and the administration's handling of it.

Heat with Some Light

A number of senators including John Danforth and a group of congressmen headed by David Dreier wrote the president to express their dissatisfaction with the way the negotiations were being handled. In early May, another group of 30 Republican senators as well as another group of congressmen, among whom Jim Kolbe played a prominent part, wrote the president to advise him that he could not count on their support for NAFTA if matters continued to develop as they were going. In the context of Leon Panetta's declaration that NAFTA was dead if prevailing conditions in Congress persisted, this move gave a jolt to the whole process. Panetta's statements were to be taken seriously; formerly a noted representative and at the time a Cabinet member (Budget Office), he understood all too well the political climate. We interpreted his remarks as a warning, not a forecast. From then on we anticipated that things would take a turn for the better. Nevertheless, on first reading, Panetta's remarks did convey contradictory impressions. Apparently he was speaking out of frustration but with the purpose of shaking the system, waking it up to the gravity of political conditions. In fact, the next day President Clinton sympathized with the feelings expressed by his budget director.

Up to that moment the whole process could probably be summarized in the headline of a *Newsweek* article on March 29 – "The Noise Is the News." This is what came across to us in the side agreements: lots of heat with no light, much noisemaking with no coherent theme.

A highly important development turned out to be an interview with Ross Perot on the Larry King Show. Abrasively and aggressively against NAFTA, Perot used a book that had been written for him, and to which he had signed his name, by Pat Choate, a noted Washington politico from whom better things were to be expected. Money is very powerful, however, and a highly unprofessional patchwork against NAFTA was put together. The main argument was based on Amerimex, the Yucatan fund that targeted as a potential buy plants that were more than 20 percent labor-intense. Choate and Perot simply stated that firms within that range would fall prey to the Mexicans and thus arrived at the ridiculous figure of 5.9 million U.S. jobs that would be lost with NAFTA. Thence the "giant sucking sound" of redoubtable memory, a shame to the person who uttered it and to the consultants who offered such a slender basis for such an outrageous conclusion. Although the argument did not hold any water, the sound bite spread like wildfire in a dry prairie.

Ross Perot directly attacked the president as well as Secretary of Commerce Ron Brown on the issue, and it became clear that the president could not avoid reacting firmly against the opinion of many politicos at the White House, lest he be perceived as caving in to the far right and the far left. Once again NAFTA had become the project that, if handled correctly, could deliver to the president a bipartisan victory—his first.

In a highly important development, seven of the most reputable of the environmental NGOs came out in favor of the agreement. Their support, although conditional, included some of the terms that provided a sound basis for a successful negotiation. Thus they accepted the notion that each country should enforce its own environmental laws rather than have others imposed. We had for a long time been trying to figure the position of the most moderate and reputable organizations and had talked to them at length. Although as a poor developing country Mexico had in the past neglected to protect its environment, it was already becoming aware of the problems created and had made sustained efforts to reverse the trend. We knew that the answer was a cooperative spirit in NAFTA rather than a big-stick attitude in the side agreements. We were thus highly relieved with the opinions we were perceiving from Laura Tyson of the EPA and from Vice President Gore, who was always highly interested in environmental problems. My Washington office gave a great deal of attention to fostering good relations with the NGOs and the associations of the environmental industry. For this task we fortunately had Raúl Urteaga, an indefatigable fighter whose actions blended strength and urbanity.

But the battle over the issue was still thriving within the White House. Ambassador Jorge Montaño of Mexico, who had replaced Ambassador Gustavo Petricioli in January 1993, publicly stated that Mexico would not enter into an agreement except under certain conditions; he implied dissatisfaction with the present and correctly spelled out the country's position. Tom Nides, the USTR office liaison with Congress, insisted that the ambassador back down or carefully add nuance to his words that would explain them away. Of course he refused.

The opposition was looking for all sorts of arguments against NAFTA. One that had already made the news was further raised by Public Integrity, an association whose title is at odds with the motivations that guide it. The organization charged that Mexico had been spending a fortune lobbying and buying influence in Washington, an accusation directed against the Office of the Free Trade Agreement that I founded and headed. The report, as well as the Perot book mentioned above, spoke highly of our organization and its professionalism; the praise was not intended to bolster our egos but to expose malevolent schemes of foreigners against the purity of national institutions.

As for the side agreement negotiations themselves, we really seemed to be in a house of mirrors. There existed, probably in all delegations, a sense of being involved in a game that confused reality and image, making it difficult to ascertain the real position of the Americans. The Mexican team had developed one plan to address the inevitable problem of financial arrangements to deal with the environmental projects, and another plan to analyze how financial measures, in lieu of sanctions, would be channeled to a common fund for border cleanup. This scheme, which was presented at the chief negotiators' meeting at the Ashby Inn, was very well crafted, and the Americans appreciated that. But they asked their counterparts to avoid its official presentation until they had had the opportunity to sell the gist of the concept to their government. We did not know what to make of this. Was this a game of mirrors, or a tactic designed to take possession of a good idea, or a gimmick to sell an idea that, in coming directly from Mexico, would not have been accepted on its own merits by people with a macho attitude toward us?

Aghast, we sent several messages to the White House that on our side negotiations were about to break down. It was already June, and little progress had been made. A new complication arose on June 15 when the administration in Ottawa changed, and Mrs. Campbell replaced Premier Mulroney as head of the Conservative Party and government. Canadian politics were playing at a different rhythm. The beleaguered Mulroney had had NAFTA approved in Parliament, and three weeks later by the Senate, before the side agreements had shown any sign of being concluded. This action was full of meaning. On the one hand it was his way of ensuring NAFTA from the Canadian side and his own authorship, and on the other it was a reminder to the United States that the agreement was the important thing, not the side agreements, which anyway were a political sideshow. Within the Canadian system, the action by Parliament would not become effective until royal assent was granted, which would come later on at the pleasure of the government.

By the end of June, no significant progress had been made. A dull wind prevailed, and the sails of our ships lay flat. According to a leak at that time, a meeting at the National Economic Council, with David Gergen as new director of communications following George Stephanopoulos, had established that all communications relating to NAFTA would be controlled by the White House. This action gave some hope of coherence to an otherwise unfocused process.

Meanwhile, a parallel issue that gravely threatened to undermine the process was being played out in the judicial branch. In late October 1992, three NGOs had sued the U.S. government for infringing the National Environmental Policy Act (NEPA), which requires the government to prepare a formal environmental impact statement before proposing any legislation that would significantly affect the environment. Public Citizen, Friends of the Earth, and the Sierra Club challenged NAFTA for not including such a statement; although President Bush had presented an Environmental Action Plan, it did not—and never intended to—fulfill the requirements of NEPA. The case was heard before Judge Charles Richey in District Court in Washington, D.C. The U.S. government, as defendant, argued that such an obligation interfered with the president's power to conduct international negotiations. On June 30, 1993, the judge decided against the government and ordered it to prepare the required statement. This action was tantamount to killing NAFTA, because preparing such a document would require an enormous amount of time. Meanwhile, opposition would grow, and the window of opportunity would be lost. Even Senator Baucus, who had always been a strong backer of environmental concerns and their implication on trade agreements, stated: "The process of conducting an Environmental Impact Statement (EIS) . . . can drag on for years. Such a long delay may endanger the international political consensus necessary. . . ."

On July 2 at the District of Columbia Court of Appeals, the government urged prompt consideration and oral arguments for the month of August. We were shell-shocked by Judge Charles Richey's decision and followed with our lawyers the various legal options available to the president should the appellate court uphold the judge's decision. There were several, but all involved much time or political risk. They ran from judicial solutions of appeal to the Supreme Court, to executive branch solutions with the president asserting his clear constitutional authority and submitting the legislation of NAFTA to Congress. In any case, the ensuing legal and political battles would have doomed NAFTA. We were somewhat relieved when, on the oral arguments in front of three judges, we found, from the tenor of their questions, that they would probably be leaning toward the administration. Finally, to our great relief, on September 23, the court decided not to sustain the District Court's decision, and we were freed from yet another deadly danger.

The Settlement

Negotiations continued, and only during the Washington's August heat with Congress already in summer recess was a settlement reached. The final weeks of negotiations were extremely difficult. The problem lay in the business of imposing trade sanctions on a country with a proven pattern of not enforcing its own laws. For some people sanctions seemed to be the only thing that mattered. In the midst of the August negotiations, Senator Baucus and Congressman Gephardt reiterated in a letter to Mickey Kantor that trade sanctions were the only effective means to force countries into abiding by their own rules.

Mexico had proposed a different and in our view effective and inoffensive system of sanctions, as mentioned above: fines paid by delinquent governments would fund a program to remedy precisely the problems at fault. Another option was to require delinquent firms themselves to pay fines if they did not adequately observe existing regulations. These sanctions as proposed by the Gephardt group were conceived more to hurt than help and provided a crack to admit protectionist interests.

During those days before the August recess, the president's economic package was finally voted on in Congress. President Clinton had put together a package that somehow mirrored his campaign promises with some help for the middle class and a deficit reduction. The package had minor tax increases for higher income levels but smelled very much of the typical "soak the rich" attitude of liberal Democrats. The White House, as much as we could tell from following rumors, was being pulled apart by internal conflict, and the battle for the legislative vote was tempestuous and wholly partisan. All Republican House members had broken with the president on the issue. A victory was in doubt until the last moment when a Democratic representative from Pennsylvania, Marjorie Margolies, cast a highly risky vote—given her predominantly Republican district—that ended the deadlock. The vote was 218 for and 216 against. The Senate fight was still worse, with a 50–50 tie that was only broken by Vice President Gore, casting his vote as president of the Senate. The slim margin of victory and the way in which it had been tortuously achieved, with the president begging for individual votes and being crossed by people he would have relied upon, were bad omens for NAFTA. Many were left wondering about the leadership of Clinton, who unlike Lyndon Johnson had problems forcing people's hands and had apparently caved in to assorted demands by members of Congress. Although this may be an exaggeration, the perception was quite real, and we had to address this pattern of internal disarray in the White House and unlimited demands in the Congress up to the ratification of NAFTA.

On August 6, the very same day of the economic package's bitter victory in the Senate, an agreement was apparently near. Two final outcomes were proposed for the end of complicated dispute-settlement procedures, after fines had been imposed without remedying the situation—a quite unlikely occurrence. There would be an alternative of either seeking redress from the offending country in its own courts, or depriving it of several limited commercial benefits arising from the agreement. Canada objected seriously, brought the issue to the Cabinet on Monday, August 9, and when no solution was found, took it finally to Parliament. The negotiations were almost abruptly suspended. Mexico was in a bind because its own legal system did not permit another country to file suit in its courts. Separate treatments would probably have to be specified for Canada and the United States, on the one hand, and for Mexico on the other. Finally a compromise was reached that required the final approval of the presidents. President Clinton had gone to Colorado to meet with Pope John Paul II, who was presiding over a big rally of Catholic youth. The president talked to Rep. Gephardt, who at the last minute issued a demand for a policy to link Mexican wages with increases in productivity. There seemed to be no end to Gephardt's demands and his attempts to run the negotiations from Congress. Luckily, Mexico had no problems with that, because a similar principle was an established policy, and Gephardt was on board. In a late-night conversation, Presidents Salinas and Clinton spoke by phone that Thursday, one year and one day after the agreement negotiations had ended, and agreed to the concepts defined by their negotiators. Hard work throughout that night made it possible for the relevant documents to be ready for public distribution the next morning.

During the negotiations, the fight to have legitimate concerns prevail and to sort out those that were protectionist, big-brother-oriented, or ignorant was continuously difficult. But the substance of the outcome worked to solve the problems we had been facing. The Labor Commission could consider issues relating to health and safety conditions in the workplace to the extent that patterns of nonenforcement of its own laws were ascertained. Countries will make their best efforts to arrive at better and comparable standards relating to those issues. The emphasis is on mutual exchange of information, technical assistance, and transparency of labor regulations, in an all-encompassing spirit of cooperation. General principles were established—for example, freedom to associate, to negotiate collectively, and to strike. The agreement defines a cooperative effort without undue interference in another's internal matters. Thus the locus of cooperation resides at the National Administration Offices (NAO) in consultation with the International Labor Organization (ILO), which had been initially opposed by the United States. In spite of the emphasis on cooperation, disputes may arise. These are limited to the nonenforcement of health and safety standards as well as child labor and minimum wage laws. A panel may convene to define whether a pattern of noncompliance exists and then propose a plan to remedy the situation. Willful misrepresentation of a panel's recommendations may be cause first for the imposition of financial penalties and then for trade sanctions within certain established limits.

In the case of the environment, the final outcome provides a well-balanced approach where cooperation to achieve a better protection of nature is related to free trade through the concept of sustainable growth. No distortion of free commerce or the establishment of trade barriers under the guise of environmental protection will be allowed. Areas of cooperation include technical assistance, education, development of needed information, and research on the most effective norms to apply. It is of great importance that individuals and NGOs are granted access to present complaints about possible violations, although only recognized entities will have access to administrative and judicial procedures. An annual report will be drafted by the Environmental Commission, and social groups may participate in an advisory committee set to advise the council on subjects pertaining to environmental problems as defined in the agreement. Whereas the scope of public participation is very large, care was taken to avoid undue interference by protectionist and radical elements in initiating legal suits that would create a deleterious, litigious approach. It is only the signatories themselves that may request the dispute settlement procedures be put in motion. This operates in a manner similar to the labor agreement.

Although the labor and environmental agreements resemble each other closely, they are not mirror images, but instead share a family likeness and certain common traits. The state of labor relations and the functioning of labor rights and trade unions are by nature deeply ingrained in a country's political and social fabric. Although cooperation is envisaged in a wide array of worker rights, the scope is limited, the system is based on local NAOs, and the issues for a dispute settlement process are narrowly defined. The approach to environmental problems is more ample and flexible. To begin with, there is large scope for the intervention and participation of various groups and individuals. The initiation of judicial procedures foreseen is nevertheless a prerogative of the signatories. Account was thus taken of the diverse nature of the two issues dealt with in the context of a free trade agreement. Only those aspects related to trade in various manners will be considered.

Although the agreements are balanced and efficient, the acrimonious way they were arrived at in the final days of negotiations provided a bitter atmosphere. On Friday morning, an agreement was announced, but later in the day Leader Gephardt apparently reneged on his offer to President Bush and jumped off the wagon, saying he would not favor NAFTA and thereby double-crossing his president and raising the odds for the passage of NAFTA. What we had always feared, and continuously tried to have members of the U.S. team understand and accept, had happened. They could not negotiate with an eye on Gephardt's nod as they had done.

If the end of the negotiations one year earlier had been a joyous occasion, with the three teams celebrating with champagne at the Watergate Hotel, this time we had a sad victory without celebration—and not only because of the Gephardt letdown, about which we were, at the moment, ignorant.

4

The Ratification

The agreement that had evolved could be called Clinton-NAFTA to distinguish it from the earlier Bush-NAFTA version. In the process the whole complex interrelationship between the three countries had been enhanced. Certainly to combine the Bush and Clinton versions created an internationally recognized agreement that was deeper and more progressive. The problem now was how to sell it.

My concern was the U.S. Congress. Canada had already approved it during the side agreement negotiations, although it was still subject to the royal assent once the new liberal government so determined. The Mexican congress on its own had yet to grant approval, but that was not directly my concern. My objective and my team's was to support approval by the U.S. Congress.

Polishing It Up

Several important legal definitions were needed, especially related to the way the side agreements would be integrated into NAFTA, whether in the implementing legislation proper or by special executive action. It had been decided it would be the former, and the putting together of the implementation legislation had already started with the USTR offices as the ones mainly responsible in continuous consultations with the Congress. For our part, the Mexicans had to study the wording of the legislation to ensure that it appropriately reflected the agreement's contents—a lengthy process involving many lawyer-hours. The Mexican legal team was headed by a sharp young lawyer with an amiable spirit of cooperation, Guillermo Aguilar Alvarez. He stayed in Washington a couple of months to review the whole process.

We had serious problems understanding the intricacies of U.S. legislation regarding the agreement. In Mexico, the agreement would acquire the status of a treaty and as such would legally supersede any provisions conflicting with it. In the United States, the agreement itself would not be voted upon and would have no legal stature. The implementation bill would be enacted into law, and any provision in the agreement itself that conflicted with existing law would have no effect. The president would have to submit to Congress the final legal text of the agreement, a draft implementing bill, a statement of any administrative action proposed to implement the bill, an explanation of how these would affect current U.S. law, and a statement on how the agreement served the interests of U.S. commerce.

Aside from the asymmetric legal status of the agreement in both countries, a further consideration involved the side agreements themselves. They were not part of NAFTA itself, which had been signed in December 1992 even before the side agreement negotiations had started. But even as a candidate, the president had viewed the side agreements as an integral part of NAFTA, so *were* they? It was confusing not just for Mexicans unaccustomed to the nuances of legal thinking in the United States, but for U.S. politicians as well. If the side agreements were not a part but simply an executive agreement, they were not subject to the fast-track procedures and could therefore be amended. Before a hearing, Mickey Kantor himself apparently said as much in answer to the questions of Republican Bill Archer. Kantor later had to clarify his position. We took some solace from knowing that we were not much worse at grasping the intricacies of the system than a noted lawyer directly responsible for these proceedings.

Yet the most important issue by far was the political task of engineering ratification in Congress. During the whole process, the Office for the Free Trade Agreement in Washington, which I headed, had been in touch with the reactions of Congress. We had with the help of the five lobbying firms followed the development of the issue along the whole negotiation process and were fairly well acquainted with the mood in Congress. The 103rd Congress was markedly different from the one that had passed the fast-track legislation in 1991. The 124 new members–110 at the House and 14 at the Senate–presented a big question mark. The Republican gain of 10 additional members reflected the more conservative, nationalistic wing of the party. Nevertheless, the Democrats still controlled both House and Senate with 258 and 57 votes respectively. The Congress had started considering an agenda derived from President Clinton's electoral campaign. The stormy final passage of his economic package and the continuous delays in presenting his health care proposals revealed the president's weak handling of a Congress controlled by his own party. Because we needed a strong president to manage his own team in Congress, we had misgivings.

The new members required our special attention, and to many of them we presented our case directly and with the help of allies. Our tally in May 1993 was of roughly the same number–33 and 32–favoring or opposing the agreement in the Senate, while 45 had expressed no opinion. Overall conditions appeared before summer to be quite balanced in the House, with 152 members favoring NAFTA and 152 leaning toward opposition or squarely opposing it. The fight would be for the 128 undecided members. We had collected valuable information about members' districts and started gathering information about the most important organizations, media, and corporations that could influence their positions. Eventually these efforts proved invaluable in campaigning for the necessary votes.

Summer Storm

Conditions became less propitious. Something had happened to tilt the balance away from what we had perceived in May. In July, according to our count, 159 members clearly favored or leaned toward NAFTA, 182 opposed it. Thus as the side agreement negotiations were drawing to a close and the actual battle for Congress loomed, we were starting at a disadvantage and had to recoup lost terrain. Mexican authorities were obviously rather concerned by our count, but we in Washington tried to assuage their fears with an extremely reasonable consideration that proved to be wrong. As yet undecided members, I explained, were more likely to come to our side because they had been subject in the past only to pressure from the opposition with little countervailing efforts by forces favoring the accord.

An alternative way of predicting the final outcome was to compare 1991's fast-track vote with the 1993 fast-track vote (just when the side agreement negotiations were most heated) that extended authority to continue negotiations with the GATT members. Although the analysis was interesting, and finally quite accurate, we gave more credence to our direct reading of the members' positions in the changing political climate. According to our analysis, 99 Democrats voted for both the NAFTA-related and the GATT-related fast track. These members would probably vote for the NAFTA agreement at the end because they were apparently trade-inclined. We thought we could get about 20 more from the ranks of the freshmen who had not voted in 1991 and others to raise a total of about 100 to 110. On the Republican side, we had 144 members of the House voting yes in both fast-track votes. Consideration of freshmen votes not included in the above and of some persons leaning against the NAFTA agreement for other than trade-related reasons led us to think that we could count on 145 Republican votes, which, added to the estimated minimum number of Democrats, would give us a handy majority of 245. Nevertheless, we relied more upon our direct vote-intention count—and that of others—which were certainly disturbing as compared to the above theoretical analysis.

For a long time the Congress had been almost delivered to the opposition. During the negotiations of the agreement proper, there obviously could not have been any plan to persuade congressmen and senators about the benefits of an agreement that did not yet exist. The administration could not do it, nor could the private sector. The Mexicans could do no more than explain the benefits an agreement would generate and the deep reforms the Mexican government had undertaken to modernize its economy and society.

During the side agreement negotiations, our efforts to promote NAFTA as more than a concept were similarly curtailed because the interest of members of Congress was on the vagaries of the negotiations. But the opposition was not impeded by any such considerations – the labor unions, the extreme environmentalists, radical groups of various sorts, and last, but certainly not least, the Ross Perot followers had taken over the corridors of Congress. During errands to Congress, several times I met Perot walking along briskly with evident self-importance, basking in the attention of eyes fixed upon him. Although I was tempted several times to address him, my temptation was easily controlled.

Much of our effort in the intervening period had been simply to carry the torch and keep it burning. We did this by staying close to the Republicans who had been and probably would continue to be the core of our support. With Democrats controlling both the White House and Congress, Republican support of NAFTA threatened to disintegrate. There was little to hold them together, and the Democrats in the administration were almost too keen to count them off. We supported many of them from our office with fact sheets, a continuous flow of information, visits to Mexico, and appointments with Mexican officials – we obviously did not pay the bills for that. A way to keep the fire alive without turning it into a controversy was demonstrated in a Tennessee campaign between Representatives Jim Cooper and Dale Johnson. Representative Cooper told us he would support NAFTA if during the campaign Johnson agreed to favor NAFTA and would refrain from making it a campaign issue. This agreement, when achieved, ensured one vote while avoiding confrontation.

Our argument – that the undecideds in Congress were more likely to favor NAFTA if they had not succumbed to the unrivaled pressure of the opposition – was sound but based on certain things remaining equal. And things did not remain equal. What was different was the rabid campaigning of the Perot crowd. We had hoped that the negotiations would be finished before Congress adjourned for the summer. We needed time to persuade members of Congress about the benefits of NAFTA before they returned to their districts to face uncertain conditions but certain attacks of the Perot contingent. We had no luck. When Congress recessed, the negotiations were not finished nor had we been able to present our case. A persistent and ominous erosion of potential support continued during August.

The most threatening period was in September when Congress reconvened. By early October according to our determinedly conservative count, we had lost 12 representatives to the undecided or leaning-against segment. The opposition had gathered 11 new members. In the Senate, conditions did not seem as bad; we estimated the support of 41 senators with 39 against and the rest remaining undecided. Our estimates became more frequent but did not improve much. By October 3 our count was 157 for and 184 against. From October 4 to October 18, we acquired 11 that were definitely favorable, out of which we had already counted 10 as leaning toward. To our chagrin, the opponents fared better: during the same period, they accumulated 23 new votes out of which 11 had been previously undecided. Things would get worse. According to Rep. David Bonior, democratic deputy leader and opposition leader, our opponents had 210 votes, which we considered an exaggeration. But the number could amount to an ominous 190–too close for comfort. Our only remaining hope was that we were losing the hard core and that a final well-concerted campaign by the administration would turn over the scales. Some potentially favorable votes could be holding out for last-minute concessions from the president, given his perceived lobbying habits.

Attitudes in Congress reflected public perception, and public perception is fickle. One of the strange surprises we encountered in the United States was the pervasive "plebiscitary" democracy determined by, and fed by, the importance of opinion polls. As I had understood it from my student days, the United States is a representative democracy whose founding fathers had established a system accountable to the people but capable of decisions based on more than the vacillations of public opinion. The president is still elected by an electoral college; the senators were initially elected by their local legislatures. Democracy means accountability. The welfare of the people is not always clear to the man in the street who cares about his daily concerns without having to have an informed opinion about every happening in the country. That is why professional politicians exist as managers for the public interest. People are the stockholders, but stockholders cannot be asked about every detail in the administration of a firm. Those decisions should be left to the managers, who will be judged by their constituents—the stockholders—on the results of management's decisions. It thus seemed to me a perversion of democracy to have a government run by opinion polls.

The advent of media has transformed all that, however. People are asked not about their opinions but about their feelings. Feelings are changing and dangerous if not guided by informed personal opinion or the opinions of trusted leaders. In my view, a failure of leadership has created a vacuum that has been taken over by the polls. On several occasions I have talked with members of Congress who referred to opinion polls as their reason to waver and remain undecided. I responded—and deeply believe—that they had been elected because they were community leaders and that a leader frames opinion and is not led by it.

Be that as it may, the prevalence of opinion polls and their impact must be treated as political reality. And we were in trouble. By February 1993, according to our opinion survey analysts Hamilton and Staff, U.S. voters favored NAFTA by a narrow 22 to 17 percent margin with about two thirds (61 percent) of the electorate unable or unwilling to evaluate the treaty. The most important aspect was the lack of opinion, even though NAFTA had been an issue in the Bush-Clinton political campaign. U.S. voters were most willing to support NAFTA when presented with arguments that stressed the benefits to the U.S. economy in terms of jobs won and consumer prices held down. Also important were arguments that stressed the advantage the United States would enjoy in terms of competition with Europe and Asia.

Yet the groups opposing NAFTA argued their position more intensely than the people favoring NAFTA argued theirs. An important factor was that after voters were informed about President Clinton's support for the negotiations of the side agreements, support for NAFTA increased dramatically to more than three to one in favor. We were thus convinced about the importance of the president's direct involvement, and for my part, I found it reassuring that Americans seemed somewhat more inclined to follow their elected leaders than their talk-show hosts—although Rush Limbaugh for our luck favored the agreement.

A balanced reading of various opinion polls is difficult because their questions are phrased in different ways, but public opinion seemed to go against NAFTA from May through September 1993. In August a CNN-USA Today poll gave figures of 44 percent against and 41 percent for; in September the figures were 41 percent against, 35 percent for. Awareness had shifted because the number of people with no opinion had shrunk considerably, but still the trend went against our interests. The difference was Ross Perot.

We had to reconsider our strategy and focus on the issues of utmost relevance. Our first strategy had been based upon an analysis made in early 1992. At that time, given severe dissatisfaction with the economy and with the leadership of President Bush, people were quite sensitive to any suggestion that the agreement could cause job loss. They were more susceptible to rejecting potential bad news without sufficiently weighing other arguments. The cons persuaded people most, as had come out in an April 1991 poll (to us, one of dubious origin) carried out under the auspices of the AFL-CIO. But we checked it with our own resources the following year and found it to be essentially correct. Although we had been first inclined to reject offhand the validity of claims by the opposition, we learned to pay attention to them. I thought that we were acting more fairly and democratically than the opponents who used all possible, even malicious, arguments.

Because we initially thought that the NAFTA debate had no great public interest, we had tried to avoid raising its profile. Trade arguments can be confusing. The debate increased, reaching a pinnacle in October–November 1993, but just a month earlier, in September, the "Times-Mirror News Interest Index" about public interest and awareness of the news placed the NAFTA debate sixth in the national interest, after the health care plan, the Amtrak train wreck, the Florida tourist murders, and the Middle East peace accords. Ominously, the same index found that those following the debate most closely viewed the treaty much more negatively than those who paid less attention. NAFTA was opposed by a 46 percent to 36 percent margin among people who followed the story very closely. Jobs formed the more potent issue in the debate, according to that survey. But it also revealed a lack of information of even those following the debate closely, because most respondents—45 percent—believed that Mexico sells more goods to the United States than the other way around. What can you do with an ill-informed public opinion reacting out of fear?

The persons favoring NAFTA—and certainly the Mexican group—stressed their support in general macro terms. Opponents used specific problems as arguments—for example, Mexican sociopolitical conditions or wildly exaggerated claims about the disastrous consequences of NAFTA approval. We could not similarly misinterpret or exaggerate problems in the United States. We could not in turn point our fingers at corrupt political mafias in several sections of the country or at the mishandling of workers in poultry cleaning plants.

Our strategy therefore was to avoid responding to, as well as initiating, attacks, which required us to develop a thick skin—a particularly difficult task for us Mexicans, with our cultural sensitivity to inappropriate or demeaning language. Our problem was to define the positive messages needed at the time and to support our cause with as much information as we could. We focused our efforts on several key states—California, Florida, and Texas—and with the help of allies, developed regional/sectoral plans to win support, for instance, from congressional members in the textile regions of the Southeast. In California we encouraged our friends to set up coalitions in key districts to focus on particularly difficult but strategic places like San Diego, which combined symbolic meaning, given its closeness to the border, with an apparently anti-NAFTA majority opinion.

We ourselves could not directly sell NAFTA to Americans. They would give us no credibility, and reactions would be negative. This was a job for the U.S.-NAFTA Coalition, for Hispanic associations friendly to the agreement, and for public officials, starting with the cabinet secretaries who were assigned several states to canvass. They would encourage grass-roots movements to influence the Congress. Our task was to develop messages, to talk and write about Mexico, and to encourage op-ed writers to discuss these issues positively. We created a matt service to provide information to newspapers about NAFTA problems, about the benefits of trade, and about Mexico as a modernizing land of opportunity.

Defining our messages was critical. The real argument for the free trade agreements, which is difficult to convey, lies in the merits of industrial specialization and rationalization. If Mexico produces a better, smaller one-door refrigerator than the United States, given its specialization in that market, and the United States manufactures a better, larger two-door refrigerator, trading will benefit everybody.

On September 21, 1993, Leader Gephardt gave a speech on NAFTA that misconstrued or distorted the facts and epitomized the following arguments of the opposition: "El Pacto," a social contract established and renewed yearly in Mexico to fight inflation among business, labor, and government, is wrong, despite the fact that many countries have used similar instruments in special cases, like the Netherlands and Spain. Wages must be raised in Mexico, as if you could do it by decree without considering supply and demand. Mexican labor productivity is high — which is certainly true in assorted cases on a plant-to-plant basis but not if you take account of the drag that an inefficient underdeveloped system puts on overall productivity. The fact is that conditions in Mexico, although already improving, would improve still more, providing an ample market and a good partner to the United States. The message of improving U.S. exports, while true, had to be treated with caution. Things are not one-sided, although people tend to view them that way. To buy U.S. goods, Mexico has to have resources, and the only stable way to acquire them is to sell to the United States.

I used to talk about the positive and negative arguments for NAFTA the way medieval mystics used to present arguments to prove God's existence. The absence of God is a proof of the need for the presence of God. I was quoted several times in newspaper articles and books on this original idea, which was sometimes repeated but not understood. The best way to put it was in terms of an improvised talk Secretary Serra gave before the president of Mexico in San Francisco on September 20, 1993:

> If you want a more polluted common border, say no to NAFTA. If you want more migration of Mexicans to the United States and to California, say no to NAFTA. If you want a less competitive North American region, say no to NAFTA. If you want to miss an opportunity that opens once in a generation chance to improve a historically difficult relationship between neighbors, say no to NAFTA.

Skeptics were more likely to accept the argument that NAFTA would increase U.S. competitiveness vis-à-vis the Asian and European economies. In fact, Mexico would be competing much more with Asia than with the United States. They also tended to accept the arguments, if made forcefully, that NAFTA would create jobs in the United States, open markets for U.S. goods, and reduce illegal immigration.

An argument I frequently used was that—*dato et non concesso*—the opposition's argument's if true held little significance anyway, given a Mexican economy less than one-twentieth the size of the U.S. economy and Mexican imports a meaningless 0.047 percent of U.S. GDP. Even the most improbable scenario—that Mexico would double its exports to the United States in five years without increasing its imports from it—would amount at most to a negligible 0.1 percent of GDP, scarcely an amount to lose sleep over or threaten the United States with the "sucking sound" of jobs being lost that Perot predicted.

Several other machines started working efficiently on the side of the angels—which was obviously our side. The U.S. NAFTA Coalition of the private sector began a very effective campaign, and most important, the White House took over the NAFTA cause as its own against persistent opposition from some of the politicos and more liberal-oriented staff. These efforts finally brought victory, but they were more than minimally supported by the efforts of the Mexican Washington office.

The office's activities had changed from lobbying and public relations during the fast track to strategic positioning during the negotiations. After nearly three years of working continuously on different aspects of one issue, we had accumulated a great deal of experience on Congress itself and the various forces and conditions involved. We had come a long way since our December 1990 draft letter answering Congressmen Don Pease and Terry Bruce in legalistic and formalistic terms, betraying a novice's understanding of U.S. political life. A staff of 20 people – including administrative assistants – with a team of one important legal firm, five lobbying firms, one public relations agency, one trade consultant, and three Hispanics representing different shades of opinion within the community, gave us understanding and confidence to support the key players with counsel and information. We never thought of ourselves as defining agents in the process, but we fulfilled a function quite vital to the success of the overall mission.

We kept our office organization flexible to accommodate changing conditions over time. The principal element was the Strategy Committee, to which we had invited persons of the caliber of Senator Bill Brock – the former senator from Tennessee, former secretary of labor, former U.S. Trade Representative, and former chairman of the Republican National Committee. Dr. Charls Walker, deputy secretary of the Treasury under various secretaries, a man with insight into the political process and an experienced analyst of the economy, was a member as was Tom Bell, the brilliant head of Burson-Marsteller in Washington, a man of great creativity and energy. Ambassador Lalo Valdez, a prominent member of the Hispanic community, former chief of protocol at the White House, and one of the first people to talk openly about a free trade agreement between the United States and Mexico, gave us judicious opinions, and Joe O'Neill, former aide to Senator Bentsen, proved to be a singularly adept person with his innate political instincts and lucid mind.

Several publications referred to me as the trainer and manager of the team and to Bob Herzstein as the quarterback. The analogy has its merits. I certainly relied upon Bob's advice in all aspects of our operation. He guided us reliably, prudently, and courageously through the intricacies and complications of the game we were playing.

Other committees were more operational in nature, such as the congressional committee comprising our lobbying team and headed by Felix Aguilar, a Mexican. Aguilar, who had first become acquainted with the U.S. Congress in late 1990, had mastered the intricacies of congressional committees. He maintained personal contact with key staff people and became an unsurpassed human database. We had retained the services of several government relations firms. Active participants in our congressional team were the above-mentioned Joe O'Neill and the Republican Phil Potter, a person with an enviable ability to analyze complex political events and offer prudent advice. With an Irish sense of humor, Bob Keefe was not only a delightful member of our team but a man of great savvy and ability to coin splendid phrases of political wisdom. Gabe Guerra, a Puerto Rican known all over town with his silver hair but youthful looks, unstintingly contributed with his "contrarian" position that created lively arguments and always shed light. Howard Liebengood, former sergeant at arms in the Senate with his intimate knowledge of the people and the workings of Congress, took a no-nonsense approach that put things back on track when diverse points of view led us astray. Kip O'Neill, son of the former House Speaker Tip of "all politics is local" memory, provided in his gentlemanly manner and deep voice an unsurpassed, balanced insight into the sense and meaning of congressional activities. His partner Andy Athy spoke little but compensated with the depth of his remarks that were always to the point.

We thus had a formidable group of people to counsel and assist us. Several Mexican officials were initially cagey about confiding our thoughts and discussing our plans with a variety of Americans whose job it was to sell their expertise on Congress. I defended the idea of relying on them as you would on a good, ethical lawyer. I had certainly no misgivings. A singular fact was the American trait of working together and developing a team spirit, even among people who previously had very little in common. I thought that this ability was probably cultivated early on in U.S. society as kids get together to play baseball, a sport that requires more team spirit than soccer.

Another very helpful committee that played a significant role was the public relations and media group. Two Mexicans presided over it at different times, José Treviño and Luis de la Calle. Treviño organized the whole effort, adding his sense of thoroughness, thoughtful analysis, and urbane touch. His unerring instinct for the appropriate phrase and his clarity of expression made a success of several of our brochures. I had known Luis de la Calle, who came to us from the World Bank, from early childhood; I was a close friend to his late father. He is a brilliant man with great clarity of thought and a businessman's capacity to get things done. At various times he also participated in initiating contacts with our Hispanic allies, a process we started during the fast-track period. In this task he had the invaluable help of Angela Giraldo, a person as diligent, intelligent, and reliable as could be found. A group of people from Burson-Marsteller provided continuous help. The person responsible most of the time was Richard Moore, a former Senate staffer, radio broadcaster, and writer from the Georgia heartland, who offered us unremitting support and experience. He put together the main elements of our public relations strategy and focused our efforts the right way in a suave, southern manner. His words streamed slowly but persistently and clearly out of his lips as from a Homeric hero. He was a hands-on manager of his team. Garth Neuffer helped enormously. A former media staffer for Senate majority leader George Mitchell, he brought flashes of creativity and gusto, an energetic approach, 24-hour-a-day attention to our concerns, and an almost poetic inspiration in his melodic deep voice. Edith Wilson was the brilliant energizer of the team—so rich in ideas that we had sometimes to restrain their abundance.

Our collective understanding about the position of members of Congress on this issue, which we had followed for three years, proved useful to many of our allies. Our familiarity with the workings of the U.S. political system, its grass-roots basis, and the varied interest groups composing it suggested some initiatives from our side. Ever since Perot had started his anti-NAFTA campaign, we had proposed to our American friends that a convenient opponent to him would be a renowned businessman known for defending U.S. interests, like the Chrysler Corporation's Lee Iaccoca. I discussed the idea with several friends in the private sector, both American and Mexican. The idea finally took hold; Iaccoca was recruited for the effort and had a brilliant media exposure. He came across as a forceful, straightforward, energetic American who was affirming the benefits of NAFTA in nononsense terms. Although we would have preferred he challenge Perot directly and suggested as much, Iaccoca did not think he was right for the job. Nevertheless we energetically pursued it: Perot, who had been given a free ride with many members of Congress, had experienced little direct opposition.

A Perot anti-NAFTA press conference was scheduled for June 10. The pro-NAFTA bipartisan liaison group in Congress preempted the meeting by organizing a countervailing conference with which we and our allies assisted. It was well attended by both members of Congress and the media – 17 members, mostly Democrats, were present, including such influential people as Dan Rostenkowski, Sam Gibbons, Phil Crane, David Dreier, and Bill Richardson – as were all the major networks and many news services. Rostenkowski made the opening salvo in his strong decisive manner by charging that Perot's attacks were based on prejudice, not on facts, and that the group's aim was to keep the debate focused on facts.

In spite of the great showing of the liaison group, about 60 members attended a two-hour forum on NAFTA with Perot sponsored by the House Republican Committee. Before the event, Ron Phillips of the Republican Research Committee staff was questioned on what made Ross Perot an expert on NAFTA, to which he gave the ludicrous response that Perot "was a successful businessman." A press conference was later held with several ranking Republicans present – Duncan Hunter, Gerald Solomon, Helen Bentley, and others. Although noted Republicans like former Secretary Bill Bennett had warned their party members about pandering to Perot, they were really creating a monster that would overwhelm them – and NAFTA.

The uppermost problem was persuading Congress about the

benefits NAFTA would bring the United States. But given the U.S. political system and the public debate NAFTA had generated, the politically active constituents would influence votes in Congress, and for the most part the opposition members were the active ones. We received continuous horror stories. At the time I wrote down a number of remarks by members of Congress I visited. "Every congressman has received at least 100 anti-NAFTA letters in the last month. We have received 500 alone." A Republican whose constituents were much influenced by Perot said: "We have received 900 NAFTA-no letters. It will be difficult to vote for it although I am a NAFTA supporter." Another added: "It is a jobs issue. Even pro-NAFTA members are looking for cover." Still another remarked: "It is not a question of substance but one of politics. . . . How can I vote for this agreement when I'm getting beat up so badly at home on job losses?" Some were probably exaggerated but ominous: "The letters are coming in 25 to 1 against the NAFTA, and these are not mass mailings. I come from a strong Republican conservative district. I won with 80 percent of the vote and the overwhelming number of constituents out there are opposed to the agreement. Perot has done irreparable damage." Still another: "This is a trade battle like never before. Perot, the United Auto Workers, and Ralph Nader are organized at the district level. The pro-NAFTA people are just sending in their national representatives, and that won't work." These and similar remarks, not one of them encouraging, were made from July through September 1993.

The Republicans had been the staunchest supporters of NAFTA since President Bush started the process. We were extremely concerned about Perot's taking hold of the radical populist right in the Republican Party. Something had to be done to stop what was, in our view, his panic-inducing blitzkrieg. Eventually Vice President Gore's office took the initiative, and the vice president himself bravely took on the task of confronting Perot. Some of our consultants were disturbed, as were many others. They believed the vice president would come across as stiff and distant.

I viewed it as a great opportunity, however. Perot had never been confronted directly on this issue by anybody of knowledge and standing. Having followed his raids against NAFTA and closely scrutinized his words, we knew he had no understanding of either the concept and its merits or details. Even if he had paid for somebody to coauthor a book on NAFTA, such as the unscrupulous Pat Choate, he had probably neither read it nor analyzed its contents honestly. Furthermore, we were acquainted with the story of his vagrancies as to NAFTA, which in our view he was opposing as a political expedient. Further, I believed that his thin skin would not resist the challenge of a man of stature's confronting his ignorance. At the request of Secretary Colosio, my former student and long-time friend, and later the ill-fated candidate for Mexico's presidency who would be insanely shot in March 1994 and who had made good friends with Gore when he was in charge of the country's environmental policy, we prepared copious notes that Gore appropriately and brilliantly used in his debate with Ross Perot.

We had discovered information on Mr. Perot's support of NAFTA in a speech at the El Paso Chamber of Commerce and similar remarks made in Monterrey about his business of supplying a Mexican financial institution with a computer system for futures trading. The most striking information was a brochure of the Alliance Airport that espoused the benefits of free trade. Among its advantages, it stated—with the signature and picture of Ross Perot—that the area "is highly competitive with other major metropolitan areas in terms of labor costs for skilled workers," exactly the argument he would be using to frighten people against Mexico. Referring to the logistics of selecting distribution sites, the brochure quotes a businessman stating that "another key factor [for the airport] is the maquiladora operations across the border in Mexico." At another point, the brochure states: "With the expected passage of NAFTA, Texas distributors should benefit from increased ties with Mexico." So much for business sense and political expedience.

One cold Sunday night I handed the above and other information to staffers at the vice president's residence. In the debate, the vice president showed the brochure directly before the TV cameras, to the stuttering embarrassment of Perot. Our information portrayed him as hypocritically mouthing free trade business talk with Mexico while proffering politically expedient one-liners of high impact.

The vice president, blunt and courageous in challenging Mr. Perot, had been self-composed and dignified in front of a man who lost control and was childishly disrespectful. His winning performance was probably the most significant factor to shift the balance toward NAFTA, as opinion polls taken afterward would attest.

A grass-roots campaign had always been necessary, but at this stage was urgent. But there were limitations, both legal and practical, to our involvement. We could not be active grass-roots promoters of NAFTA. Our position would be suspect; Americans would have to determine and promote the interest of the United States. But because we believed in this case that U.S. interest coincided with Mexico's, we were ready to provide whatever support we could to those associations willing to become active.

The U.S.-NAFTA Coalition, although established early on, had not been very active. Until the Bush plus Clinton negotiations were completed, the coalition could not promote a product that did not yet exist. Also, the coalition's two cochairmen had rather difficult conditions to face. Both James Robertson, head of American Express, and Kay R. Whitmore, head of Kodak, had been forced by their companies' domestic struggles to resign their positions, which left the coalition leaderless. Lawrence Bossidy of Allied Signal and Jerry Junkins of Texas Instruments took over. Their government relations officials in Washington were thus appointed to head the working of the coalition, replacing Sandra Masur of Eastman Kodak, a determined but rather conditional ally. At that time a solid structure had already developed, with "captains" appointed for the different states to promote NAFTA efforts. On that existing structure, the new heads imposed a dynamic required by the prevailing conditions. The man most engaged in directing the efforts was Allied Signal's man in Washington, Ken Coale, a person of great skill, understanding, and drive. The heads of large corporations were in general known to favor NAFTA and had already made their rounds of the corridors of Congress. What was missing was to engage the participation of the hundreds of smaller companies that would have to benefit. To corral all of them and stimulate their action was the role of the U.S.-NAFTA Coalition.

When the fast-track procedure has first started, I had received my first briefing on the complex nature of U.S. business association dealings with NAFTA from the clear and brilliant mind of Colleen Morton. The U.S.-NAFTA Coalition, the main business organization supporting NAFTA, comprised 2,300 U.S. corporations and corporate lobby groups by June 1993. It had a grass-roots organization that had appointed "captains" for each of the 50 states to convince the public that NAFTA would be good for them. Because some corporations were in charge of more than one state, 35 corporations served as captains for the 50 states. AT&T was assigned 7 states, including Florida, New Jersey, and Wisconsin; IBM had 5 states, including Alabama and Vermont; General Electric had the New England states. Other companies from across the spectrum—DuPont, Textron, Fluor, NIKE, Warnaco, and others—led the fight for NAFTA in the different states. All but one of the state captains were from the 500 largest firms. All but four of the state captains enjoyed privileged access to the NAFTA negotiation process through representation on advisory committees to the USTR and were therefore privy to the negotiations themselves and familiar with their outcome.

The U.S.-NAFTA Coalition had faced a dilemma ever since the start of the negotiations. They wanted NAFTA, but not *any* NAFTA. As the agreement itself was completed in August 1992, they started mobilizing, advising their members that a first-rate North American Free Trade Agreement was reached that was clearly in the economic interest of U.S. business, workers, and consumers. They wrote openly to their members that "opponents are already organized and have targeted defeat of the NAFTA as their number one legislative priority. They are not waiting. . . ."

Even before this, opponents had taken action in special cases as the negotiations neared their final stage in July 1992. One of several attempts to derail the whole process—Senate Resolution 109, named the Riegle resolution after its sponsor—would have

essentially eliminated fast-track procedures for congressional review. This resolution had bewildered the Mexican team and any
sense of logic. Introduced by Senator Donald Riegle on April 23,
1991, even before the fast-track vote, this simple Senate resolution, which would require neither the concurrence of the House
nor of the president, was typical of statutes containing procedural
provisions. The 1988 Trade Act, for example, which provided
the framework for the fast track, stated that those procedures are
enacted pursuant to the rulemaking power of both chambers,
each of which can establish rules governing its own proceedings.
This rulemaking, reserved under section 1103 of the Trade Act,
empowers the Senate to exercise its constitutional right to make
new, superseding rules to govern consideration of such agreements as NAFTA. For those of us educated in the Roman system
of law, this was like walking in a legal swamp where the ground
could give way at any moment.

Aside from such obvious menaces as the Riegle resolution,
the U.S.-NAFTA Coalition had not come together as a solid,
purposeful organization until the end of the side agreements.
Coalition members had been scared that Mexico would give up
too much to the requests of the liberal Democrats and were
reserving their energy. Several times some of them did not take
kindly our urging that, even so, some effort had to be undertaken
to counter organized opposition. But it did come together in
special cases like the fight against the Riegle resolution.

The Mexican team accomplished an overall and quite effective support. Months earlier we had started, with the help of
COECE, the Mexican business group for NAFTA, to establish a
list of U.S. companies that had some business relation to Mexico
as exporters, investors, providers of technology, et cetera. That
list reached 12,000 and was the product of a great variety of
Mexican companies who supplied the names of their U.S. contacts. We analyzed the location of their facilities, distributed their
headquarters and plants geographically, and then matched them
with the 150 electoral districts needing a special promotion.
These included districts of congressional members that were either sitting on the fence or even some leaning against it, but
that we thought could be brought back with the help of some

grass-roots activity. We handed our list to the coalition members, and they worked extremely well.

The imposing machinery of the private sector started gaining momentum. Coalition members visited with local executives, asking them to write, visit with, or call their representatives. An impressive array of events was planned. "Product days" were held to show states how they would benefit from NAFTA as well as "sectoral days" for agricultural, chemical, and financial industries. The campaign culminated in a White House exhibition that showed samples or models of thousands of U.S. products exported to Mexico. At least 1,500 persons attended, including workers whose living depended at least partially on those exports. Twenty TV cameras covered this successful event.

Several corporations had started their own grass-roots activities even before the side agreements ended. Some of these efforts were outstanding in their efficient organization, like the ones of the Dow Chemical Company, Bechtel, or General Electric. All this activity took place at arms-length distance from the Mexican team. The relation was purposefully rather one-sided in the sense that we provided information about congressional targets and concerns of people about NAFTA agreements and how to answer them. For instance, we analyzed the potential impact of NAFTA's provisions for different industries – for example, lumber, electronics, and insurance. We related the information to corporations with facilities in districts that were of interest to us and also provided the same information to the coalition. We never expected, however, to have direct, hands-on collaboration, and they intentionally acted quite independently, providing little or no feedback.

Our main role was to gather, analyze, and distribute information, but we participated directly in hundreds of seminars, talk-shows, and meetings with trade associations. Some people complained even at congressional hearings that we Mexican trade officials had been, in the words of Keith Bradsher of the *New York Times*, engaged in "preaching to the converted" (August 10, 1993, p. 2). This idea was echoed by Mickey Kantor, who stated at the committee that he had tried in the most vivid but polite language to pass this concern to us. As a matter of fact, we did attend meetings to which we were invited, and indeed invitations mostly came from supporters or people eager to understand. No use in discussing much with opponents. We analyzed press reports carefully to discover new allies to whom we could send fact sheets and other material. To focus our activities as sharply as possible, we analyzed cities and metropolitan areas at four different levels and determined their most influential media in order to try for invitations to editorial board meetings or to encourage our friends to write op-eds. Thus we established 11 areas as a first priority, 18 as second, 11 as third, and 28 as fourth. For example, we placed Cincinnati in our second tier because of two influential local newspapers covering an area with three members leaning toward NAFTA – one undecided and two against. Denver, Colorado, was a media center that reached the constituents of five members leaning toward NAFTA and three undecided. It was also on our second tier.

From the start of the fast-track debate, we had encountered the Hispanic community and had come to establish an ongoing relation with it. The administration in particular urged us during the last months of the debate to prioritize our contacts with them. Matters were not as simple as a first glance would suggest. The Hispanic community in the United States is a divergent group, depending on national origin (whether Puerto Rican, Mexican, or Cuban), residency status in the country (degree of permanence), or particular ethnic mix (the differences, for example, between Texan Mexicans from New Mexico or Californian Mexicans). They all share Spanish as their language and certain values related to family, friendship, and easygoing human exchange. These provide a sense of unity if considered in contrast to the U.S. community of either non-Iberian European or African traditions. But looked at in isolation, that unity is fragmented by different origins, educational levels, and a certain rabid individualism that runs through much of the Ibero-american culture. Even the Americans of Mexican descent have their own variations, and not all were brought easily to the idea of having stronger ties with Mexico through a trade agreement. Some who had left Mexico long ago because it could not provide them a decent living were quite ambivalent in their loyalty to their country. Others felt threatened if their jobs were taken away by low-wage Mexican workers south of the border. Still others were totally taken over by their efforts to integrate into mainstream America and were quite indifferent to trade policy or other ethnic considerations.

It was thus very difficult to deal with the Hispanic community as a unit. The Hispanics were integrated into different associations, some strictly political and geared to foster voter participation, others representing shared interests of the different communities and directly influencing Congress and the administration in Washington and in a variety of states. The Castro-obsessed Cubans had no understanding of Mexico's tradition of strong links with Cuba—with the historical Cuba that had been probably the closest of old Spanish colonies to Mexico, but which they interpreted as support for the communist regime. The Mexican government made this quite clear to the leaders of the Cuban community and was forthcoming in several ways, having shown courtesy and understanding to prominent members of the community, such as Mr. Mas Canosa, who certainly appreciated it but was caught between conflicting views. The economic and social policies pursued by the Mexican government showed no proclivity toward the Cuban Marxist political system. If NAFTA was approved, Cuba would certainly become part of it once Castro's regime faded away. NAFTA was therefore to be promoted. Although this was our message to them, it had little effect politically because all members of Congress of Cuban origins or sympathies voted against.

Very early in the fast-track process, we contacted the most relevant Hispanic organizations and were well received. Although the Hispanics were mostly Democrats who tended to espouse the more left-wing positions, they were sentimentally inclined to support NAFTA. They were torn, and we needed, if only for symbolic reasons, their support. Some Hispanic organizations had held back during the fast track, touting the idea that NAFTA would actually cause job loss for Hispanics. To stem this negative opinion, which we believed could pose a major obstacle to congressional approval, we had implemented a strategy from late 1991 through 1993. We talked about the bold measures Mexico had taken to become a partner in the world trading community. NAFTA would strengthen friendship and respect between the United States and Mexico, which would reflect positively upon the Hispanic community. We identified key Hispanic business, political, and civic leaders in congressional districts with a significant Hispanic population and informed them on the benefits of NAFTA. We had particularly focused on the 100 members of Congress with a significant Hispanic constituency and alerted our friends on the need to establish local coalitions. Several were established, particularly in California where the need was greatest. We provided continuous information and were personally ready to assist them.

At times I myself directly experienced rather virulent personal attacks inspired more by emotion than by analysis. The Hispanic business community was without exception extraordinarily active, well organized, energetic. I was very much impressed that their entrepreneurial spirit boded well for their U.S. community and could provide a splendid link to strengthening the difficult relations with Latin American countries.

We had been encouraged by the fact that Gov. Clinton had during his campaign invited prominent Democratic leaders of Hispanic origin to Little Rock on August 31 and that a substantial majority of those invited (73) and attending (47) were favorable to NAFTA. But this did not prove of longstanding effect. When the side agreement negotiations started, the most radical social activists were leaning toward the more radical positions, and we faced strong opposition from them.

Nevertheless, efforts were made to try to get a unified stand more favorable to NAFTA but with adequate reservations to allow for the signing in of different groups. This effort was led prominently by La Raza, probably the best-known Hispanic organization, whose President Raúl Izaguirre always actively and smoothly promoted NAFTA. Efforts to achieve a unified stand failed at a meeting in El Paso. A Latino summit was convened in Washington in March 1993. Although we had initially viewed these efforts favorably and had friends who would apply pressure for the NAFTA side, we had some reason to be apprehensive about the outcome because social activists had apparently taken over the organization. To counter this trend, the supporters of NAFTA held a news conference on March 11, the day before the summit, that included mostly Hispanic business organizations like the Hispanic Chambers of Commerce with its forceful president José Niño; the Texas American Mexican Chambers of Commerce with the enthusiastic Ernesto Chavarría, and the Border Trade Alliance with the efficient and urbane Gerry Schwebel. Most favored the passage of NAFTA "as it is written." Others, like Ada Peña from LULAC (League of United Latin American Citizens), asked to be given entree into the dialogue around the side agreements and indicated that provisions must be made for U.S. workers who may be displaced. All in all, with the help of attending Reps. Richardson of New Mexico and Bonilla of Texas, the conference was an endorsement of NAFTA aimed at influencing the next day's Hispanic summit. It proved useful, but the much-hoped-for unified position at the summit was not to be achieved. The summit had been tilted from the beginning by the make-up of the groups, which was slanted toward social activism. A concerted effort was probably made to encourage participation of the activist groups and shut out the professional groups. A document drafted and leaked to the press a day earlier with the help of Southwest Voter Registration and MALDEF (the Mexican American Legal Defense Fund) sided with the approach of the Democratic party left wing. The document raised havoc. Among the few supporters of NAFTA present, José Niño stood up and forcefully announced: "We are pro-NAFTA. Labor problems were here before NAFTA. Environment problems were here before NAFTA. . . . We remove ourselves from this process." The document was finally given to the different organizations for consideration, and the summit was, luckily, a failure. We had avoided a major embarrassment. At the end, however, a unity of sorts was achieved in Washington on the NAFTA vote, yet without including all the Hispanic members of Congress.

Our efforts to establish links with the Hispanic community were unparalleled. We visited with their leaders, had speaking engagements at their meetings, established contacts with their most prominent intellectuals and business leaders, and amplified the efforts that Mexico had already undertaken in the past, particularly through Roger González de Cossío. Their reception was always mostly warm in spite of not always being favorable to NAFTA. There were occasions when we felt extremely gratified from a personal point of view. Many Hispanics, and certainly many Mexican-Americans, were proud to be courted by a team that had negotiated at a high professional level with those Anglos who had not always in the past shown due respect for them and their traditions. The standing ovations that Secretary Serra and Chief Negotiator Blanco frequently got from Hispanic audiences were testimony to this deeply felt appreciation. In terms of voting, the final outcome of this sustained effort was mixed, because a substantial minority of Hispanic representatives voted against NAFTA. It nevertheless accomplished much by forging deep links with, and respect for, the efforts of that Hispanic diaspora that will certainly endure and grow. It was the Sanchez-Sanchez-Smith approach made popular by Secretary Serra. With NAFTA, the Hispanics would be the binding element that would make our countries prosper together.

Mexico

The administration urged us to enhance the image of Mexico. Much of the opposition to NAFTA originated from a negative image of the country, perhaps simply born out of ignorance. Stereotypes about Mexican "bandidos," illegal aliens, people in poverty, and corrupt drug traffickers cast Mexico in a light detrimental to developing an agreement. Our own opinion polls confirmed the same idea. It is an impossible task to change the image of a country—however biased—within a few years or with a media campaign. We tried not so much to dispel wrong concepts but to tell the story of the great progress Mexico had made in the recent past to become a better, more efficient, and more just society.

We were very much aware of the problems Mexico had and the reasons why we had such a bad image. A story is told by a famous Mexican cartoonist about a typical Mexican in his large hat, talking with a big, loud-voiced American who says, "In my country we speak very badly about Mexico." The Mexican answers, "In my country too!" But we saw—in a manner I hope not too biased by love of country—that Mexico had made enormous strides, that it was converting itself into a new and better society, and that NAFTA was an instrument to pursue appropriate developments as well as lock in much of what had been accomplished.

In the evenings, after a day's exhausting meetings on the side agreements at the Madison Hotel, we often went out for dinner with Secretary Serra, Herminio Blanco, and Blanco's deputy, Jaime Zabludovsky. As we relaxed, we talked about the meaning of NAFTA. We saw it as an integral part of our country's efforts to become more competitive and thus more efficient. But our conversations dwelt more on how it could become more disciplined, transparent, and just.

We were therefore deeply frustrated by the willful lack of understanding we frequently encountered. Many wanted Mexico to become in a single stroke a "civilized" country in an American sense. Many of them were simply not interested in comprehending Mexico's efforts and success, neither had they any understanding of "30 Centuries of Splendor," as the title of an exhibition on Mexican culture read. We knew that much of what the opponents said about our country was true, but it was not the whole truth. And certainly we were not fighting for an economic model that would grant more opportunities to rich Mexicans at the expense of the underprivileged.

A thing that continuously amazed me is the tendency we humans have toward inconsistency. The United States has had a highly successful record of marginal improvements in its social and political structure. Americans do not easily accept grandiose ideas that are proposed to fundamentally change a system. They are right. History shows that gradual but continuous improvement is better suited for society's development—although the reverse is also true: the accumulation of gradually accepted defects imperils society's strength. What seemed strange and confusing to me was the insistence of opposing politicians that Mexico would have to become, almost overnight, a country with no defects in its judgment. The United States itself exercised sound judgment to reject, for instance, the ambitious health reform proposed by President Clinton. Some Americans tried to impose on others attitudes and procedures they would not accept for themselves.

We finally decided against our first approach of not getting involved with mass media. We would hold a low profile, focusing a media campaign on Mexico's image to the extent needed to support other pro-NAFTA efforts. We were able to convince a group of Mexican businessmen of the need, and they agreed to finance a limited effort. Some well-focused TV and newspaper ads were prepared that went something like this: "Which country has in the past year constructed so many hospitals or schools or accomplished so many air-cleaning projects?" The obvious answer: "Mexico. Together in NAFTA we will do it still better." The data were all scrupulously real.

The advertising company brought together some focus groups to gauge the reaction of viewers and readers. I was invited to some. It was appalling to witness the amount of ignorance about Mexico and the disbelief of any good information about it. Some people asked, "Do you mean we are going to construct these many hospitals for them?" or questions of that nature. Nevertheless, after the discussion in the groups, their reaction became more positive, and the decision was made to go ahead.

As things were, we continued to try our best to promote the writing of op-eds that commented on Mexico's progress in a forthright, nondefensive way. The focus groups had given us a clue about what was actually happening: in most cases, people emerged from our speaking engagements with an improved image of what Mexico was and a positive view of what the future would bring. No better argument can be made than to see the other person as a human being and not as a sombrero stereotype. We were fighting not only against the past. At the same time, the opposition was airing some very nasty, unsavory ads, like one where you hear the sound of a crash and then a voice saying: "This will happen when Mexican truck drivers are permitted into our country." We found such ads extremely distasteful and lacking in the common courtesy one should show to another country. But they were a fact, and we had to counteract them. It was, after all, the manner in which U.S. politicians fought against each other.

White House Involvement

For some time we had entertained the idea of convening a group of eminent U.S. citizens to underwrite NAFTA. The idea first came to us during the transition of administrations from Bush to Clinton. We hoped to influence the new government with the statesmanlike opinions of respected people. We thought of former presidents and secretaries of state and the treasury, as well as other prominent politicians who had in the past been actively engaged in foreign policy and economic issues. The idea came to naught at the time, but when the side agreements were nearly completed, it returned, tilted this time not toward the administration but toward the American public. Americans might listen to people of responsibility who at the time had no particular ax to grind. I personally talked to former President Ford about this at a meeting in Colorado, and he was sympathetic. The idea gained momentum, and on October 12 former Presidents Ford, Carter, and Bush issued a strong endorsement of NAFTA, with the added support of other notable persons—James Baker III, Jeane Kirkpatrick, Edmund Muskie, George Shultz, Andrew Young, et cetera. I was particularly impressed and happy by the signing in of that great Democratic leader whose imprint still remains in the party, Tip O'Neill.

The state governors may not be directly involved in the passage of such federal legislation as NAFTA, but they see the interest of their states with a larger perspective than the more locally oriented representatives. The whole Mexican effort focused on developing relations with the governors and their economic or development departments. Many participated in missions to Mexico, and we would always make sure they would visit with President Salinas, whose charming, warm personality and grasp of the issues had the desired effect on his guests. As early as the end of 1992, 17 governors had visited Mexico, and at the end we had the invaluable support of 42 governors. We used this support extensively as an important asset to persuade the wavering.

The clue to the whole battle, however, was President Clinton. In August when the side agreements were almost ready and one would have expected some drilling for the upcoming battle, the White House kept a low profile. This was highlighted by the nonappearance of officials at a hearing on NAFTA in the Senate Commerce Committee. The White House was subject to crossfire on the issue. The president's own party was foremost in opposition, and 110 congressional Democrats had written the president to ask him to put NAFTA on hold until Congress had dealt with health care reform. The concept, in the words of the letter's proponent David Bonior, was that free trade would be divisive and should not impede the consideration of health care reform. Specious arguments like these were made by opponents hedging on perceived presidential priorities that were far less ready than NAFTA to come before Congress. These attempts were based on a misunderstanding of Clinton's commitment to NAFTA. Although the president's words had indicated his personal conviction about NAFTA's benefits to the United States, somehow he was caught within the opposition of his own party and did not give the clear signals needed. His staff, we heard, had proposed a fall schedule focused almost totally on health care with only sporadic attention to NAFTA. This changed when staunch NAFTA supporter Secretary Bentsen brought it to the attention of the president.

Doubters in the president's camp apparently included Hillary Clinton, George Stephanopoulos, Paul Begala, and David Wilhelm among others. (Some insiders who were telling us that the president's wife was against NAFTA were probably hiding behind the first lady's name because it was clearly difficult for us to find out the truth—which anyway did not matter much at this stage.) For our part we tried to convey to all players the idea we had first espoused at the beginning of the side agreement negotiations. The president would achieve a great victory by showing himself to be a bipartisan statesman who reached for the benefits of the country beyond extreme party politics. Now he had played into the hands of those extremists led by Gephardt, who had finally let him down. And further, because he had endorsed NAFTA and made it his own through the side agreements, a rejection by Congress would be a great defeat for him. The White House staff had to be more precise in calculating in advance which issues they could manage with strong Democratic majorities and which required bipartisan support. The agreement urgently needed bipartisan support and the president's strong commitment. Our hope was that Clinton's experience as governor and during the Democratic primaries showed that he was adept at rebounding from enormous setbacks once his back was against the wall.

An important and, for us, welcome drift had been occurring at the White House. Clinton's chief lobbyist Howard Paster, a man whose conversation I found extremely interesting although he was not personally committed to the cause of NAFTA, was blamed among others by Clifford Krauss in the *New York Times* of disdaining positions of the Democratic conservatives, let alone reaching for Republicans. We thought initially he was not the right champion to fight the congressional battle for NAFTA, although he later on proved to be an effective operator for the NAFTA cause. James Carville, who had been opposed and whose tactical acumen we feared, began making a subtle, well-balanced attempt to endorse NAFTA. On July 25, he wrote an interesting *Washington Post* article that, under the enticing title "Help Those Whom NAFTA Will Hurt," encouraged support for the president's worker-training programs and aid to small industries. Because pro-NAFTA forces would have to assume responsibility for the real lives of those whose jobs NAFTA would displace, this article, coming from a tactician of the inner Clinton circle, was an extremely encouraging sign that changes were occurring there.

The position of the White House's inner circle on NAFTA reminded us of the verses of Arthur Balfour, who nearly a century ago wrote:

> I'm not for Free Trade and I'm not for protection
> I approve of them both, and to both have objection . . .
> So in spite of all comments, reproach and predictions
> I firmly adhere to unsettled convictions.

Such, we thought, were the convictions of Mr. Clinton's entourage, but we hoped that beyond short-term considerations he would finally come out forcefully for NAFTA, as he had already shown he could. He came out strongly for NAFTA in September, but once again reneged in his open support owing to health care. A case in point occurred at the gala celebration of the Hispanic caucus on September 16 – coincidentally the celebration of Mexican independence. The president gave a speech, but said he understood that several of those present did not favor NAFTA. That he made such a statement without defending NAFTA strongly gave the effect of tepid support.

But anyway we did not know what to make of these apparent inconsistencies between avowed priorities and scheduled times. In a *Wall Street Journal* article of November 2, 1993, Michael Frisby and Gerald Seib put it this way:

> Why didn't Clinton and his administration convey this passion earlier? The answer seems to lie in the disconnection between his own feelings and a series of tactical political considerations that were designed to appease his dissenting friends within the party and colored his public presentations of the issues.

This had been clearly seen in the attitude of his negotiators, who catered to Gephardt and later were left out in the cold by him. A connection between his feelings and his strategy was found. The political campaign received a great thrust when Bill Daley, a Chicago lawyer of the famous political dynasty, agreed to become NAFTA czar. Yet, the very idea of the need to create a position of czar led some to suspect that the White House was internally weak on this score and could not rely on its own resources. Initially Daley, a talented man always ready to listen and judicious in his remarks, had very few people working directly for him, but he put together teams working out of several departments, among which the State Department's solid staff under Ambassador Charles Gillespie did fine work. Regions were assigned to the different departments, and in particular secretaries became directly involved calling on members of Congress and assigning them different regions of the country in which to promote NAFTA.

Things began to change. The true believers got the upper-hand in the White House as they saw that instead of winning votes we were embarrassingly losing them. It was then that the president, with the support of many others, among which certainly the orchestrator of all, Mr. Daley, started a steadfast campaign for NAFTA. President Clinton started making calls to members of Congress three times a day. He hosted luncheons with Democrats and Republicans jointly and invited some of them to accompany him on Air Force One.

The great opening bang, however, was the presentation of three former presidents in behalf of NAFTA. We had suggested as much several months before and even initially contacted some of them, as mentioned above. Mr. Carter was particularly impressive in conceding outright that there were problems in Mexico but asserting that NAFTA would help solve them. Although not a welcome message to some Mexicans, it was powerful precisely because it was blunt, honest, and not totally positive to Mexico.

President Carter had reason to understand the predicaments of NAFTA. He had lived through a politically similar acrimonious debate, the unpopular Panama Canal treaties. The anti-treaty coalition had been headed by Senator Dole—replaced in our new act by Dick Gephardt—and had Ronald Reagan as the staunchest leader outside Congress—a role taken over by Ross Perot in the NAFTA debate. Further, President Carter's Panama Canal campaign was headed by Hamilton Jordan, a role that fell upon Bill Daley. Hamilton Jordan, incidentally, was again involved in the NAFTA debate by giving sound and experienced advice about the grass-roots activity needed to influence congressional waverers into passing NAFTA.

The president started inviting groups of congressmen to the White House twice a week. He came out so far that answering to a Republican congressman, he said, and later reiterated, that he would not defend in later elections Democrats who had attacked Republicans for their support of NAFTA—a very courageous gesture that helped project the image of Clinton as a fighter making a comeback. It certainly helped NAFTA become a bipartisan issue as it should have been in the first place, and it reinforced the hand of Newt Gingrich, the newly elected future minority leader. Many Republicans had been sitting on their hands, looking at the embarrassing position Clinton was being trapped into by having made NAFTA his own through the side agreements while lacking his own party's backing. Mr. Gingrich had to demonstrate his strength against his main opponent for the leadership, Rep. Solomon, who opposed NAFTA. More important, he had to show himself capable of promoting a bipartisan policy as against his maverick partisan image, which was not conducive to a congressional leader.

Last Skirmishes

Meanwhile, the markup was going on. According to the fast-track regulations, no amendments could be accepted, but the U.S. legislative strategy has an ingenious contrivance that allows amendments to the implementing legislation. The Congress was thus able to influence the legislation itself rather than simply vote the agreement up or down. On October 18, the legislation came open for amendments. We were rather nervous lest a significant change be promoted, although we knew the administration favored having the agreement translated into legislation in the cleanest, most transparent way possible.

The more than 20 amendments proposed were significant and did disquiet us. Some had the probable intention of harassing Mexican producers of televisions sets, as the one of Rep. Jim McCrery. One recommendation appeared to mandate for the United States a managed trade policy for automobiles requiring quantitative goals in obvious contradiction with the spirit and letter of NAFTA. At least three recommendations intended to change or influence decisions of binational panels under chapter 19 and the U.S. courts. These were probably the most serious, but other proposals dealt with acceleration of tariff schedules, approval of future changes in rules of origin for textiles, modification of safeguard laws for perishable products, etc. We did not initially gauge the extent and seriousness of these proposals. They could be postures for local consumption, "fishing expeditions" to see what they could get, or simply different ways to impede the process. Our fears were groundless. The amendments proposed by Reps. Gibbons and Crane, among others, were about domestic issues arising from the agreement, but fortunately did not affect the agreement itself.

I was frequently reminded of the story of the Spaniard who had in his will established a condition for his heirs to receive the inheritance: if he died in Spain, he should be buried in Mexico, and if he died in Mexico, he should be buried in Spain. When asked the reason for such flagrant arbitrariness, he replied: "Es por joder," or loosely translated, "Just to piss them off."

Everybody was now counting votes one by one in the House, which was the first to vote and had the strongest opposition. If we passed the House, the Senate could not exactly be taken for granted, but we were confident. Some commentators say that the vote for NAFTA was a pork-barrel affair. It was not, according to my knowledge. Obviously the president promised certain people his personal help for some of their main initiatives, or sided with them on certain issues. He may also have promised his personal support and appearance during reelection campaigns. This is standard political practice, not a give-away. Several issues gave this project a wrong image. One was the National Development Bank, or NADBank, and the other was the citrus and sugar side-letters, both of which were an eleventh-hour concession of both the U.S. and the Mexican governments.

At the end of the side agreements we had no more than 70 Democrats and 110 Republicans on our side. On November 4, the president submitted the implementing legislation to the Congress, by which time we still were short by about 20 votes. The Democratic whip for NAFTA, the ebullient, forceful, and intelligent Bill Richardson had one; on the Republican side were the gentlemanly, sharp, and energetic Jim Kolbe and the charming, optimistic David Dreier. The White House office for NAFTA, headed by Bill Daley with the special support of Tom Nides from USTR, had a comprehensive vote count as did the private-sector-supported U.S.-NAFTA Coalition. We had our own prognosis, which was probably the most consistent and conservative because we had followed the positions of many members of Congress for almost three years. We had created a model to predict the outcome based on the vote for the two fast-track votes. With some variations it seemed by early November that we had a difficult task of getting a majority vote in Congress, but nonetheless we thought we were making good progress.

Our allies started looking for specific groups of legislators who had not declared themselves and who had a particular request that could probably be accommodated. One request was for the National Development Bank, which had been, in principle, established in the agreements but had not had its structures and functions defined. NADBank had been the brainchild of Rep. Esteban Torres (D-Calif.) and Raúl Hinojosa, a professor at San Diego University. Raúl Izaguirre was trying to bring a number of Hispanics to our side who were either opposed or sitting on the fence. Rep. Torres wanted 10 percent of the funds in the NADBank to be available for urban projects in cities not far away from the border. After long consultations it was finally agreed. We were confident that this effort would bring us eleven new votes. On the very day of the official announcement, we were hoping for six or seven, and finally only one, Torres, officially announced his support for NAFTA. We were disappointed about the numbers, but felt successful because Rep. Torres was known as a union supporter. He had the reputation of having a strong appreciation for Mexico, but also of having been strongly opposed to NAFTA. In time, others joined Torres in their support.

With the NAFTA showdown approaching, we had already experienced what it would mean in the sense of final horse-trading. We were initially appalled until we learned the U.S. rules of the game and how many proposed trade-offs were totally irrelevant to the arguments discussed. This is part and parcel of the pragmatic U.S. system. On things that do not matter to you, but where people need your vote, you simply come out with sometimes outrageous and frequently unrelated claims that are the cost of your vote. It is a form of democratic bribery. In Mexico we were used to bribery as the result of an inadequately paid civil service, corruption in the political leadership, and an inefficient system that sometimes works more rapidly with the use of unethical incentives. We were not proud of it. What I found in the United States, however, was a different kind of bribery. Although it was mostly legal, it was similar in that it called for using–or abusing–one's power to receive benefits.

Rep. Clay Shaw brought up the case of extradition for a man who supposedly had raped a four-year-old girl. Several representatives defended a Mr. Wilkerson, a U.S. archaeologist who had been granted rights to uncover a site in Veracruz he had discovered, against prior claims by some Mexicans. Rep. Donald Manzullo brought up the case of a Campos family, probably constituents of his who had been traveling by car in Mexico. The car had been taken away by the police because the driver was a disallowed person. (In Mexico, a car with a foreign license cannot be driven by a Mexican resident.) Many people thought the NAFTA argument in Congress permitted them to introduce irrelevant, tangential issues. This was also the case when a group of 39 U.S. trade unionists entered Tijuana on a tourist visa but proceeded to proselytize opposition to NAFTA among workers of maquiladoras. Mexican police brought them to the immigration office, and they were informed they should not engage in such activity. They returned to the United States and, with the story of having been detained and harassed, confirmed their worst fears about NAFTA. They reported this story to various members of Congress, without mentioning that they had been involved in an illegal activity in the first place.

The concerns raised were varied. Rep. Tom Lantos held a number of hearings about apparent corruption when IBM was not granted a contract by Mexican airport authorities and several times had Mr. Moussavi, an Iranian of dubious reputation, as the main witness. Other hearings of the House Subcommittee on International Security and Western Hemisphere Affairs were held on Mexico's records on human and worker rights with abundant participation of social activists. Ralph Nader and Jesse Jackson testified before the House Government Operations Subcommittee on Employment with chairman John Conyers presiding. They predictably blasted Mexico. I had breakfast with Reverend Jackson some time earlier and discussed his possible endorsement of NAFTA. He had been disarmingly open to the fact that it would depend upon the business opportunities that it would bring for the black community. Such set-asides were out of the question, and he proceeded to oppose NAFTA and threaten demonstrations at plants that might lose jobs to Mexico.

Ever since the negotiations ended in 1993, some sectoral issues remained unresolved to the satisfaction of groups with political clout. They included the sugar producers, whose support was mostly in the Florida and Louisiana delegations; the citrus and vegetable producers of Florida; several industries producing flat glass like PPG and Guardian, whose support was mostly with Reps. Phil Crane and Arno Houghton; several companies based mostly in Iowa that wanted to accelerate the elimination of tariffs on home appliances. These and other interests were working hard to push for a last-minute letter of understanding in effect modifying the agreed-upon text. Several of these were encouraged by the apparent support of Mickey Kantor, who insisted on a redefinition of fructose and sugar, on special safeguards for citrus, and on the acceleration of tariff reduction for a number of these and other products. We were extremely sensitive to this because any reinterpretation was tantamount to reopening, and there would be no end to this process once unleashed.

If you had to pick up a number to put you over the hump, a rather obvious choice would be congressmen with strong ties to sugar and citrus interests, sectors traditionally protected and having formidable political and economic influence. This happens, among other reasons, because those interests are concentrated in a few areas and with their great clout may carry a disproportionate weight in state caucuses. Such was the case in Florida and Louisiana. From the very beginning this group had been opposed to NAFTA. At the negotiations two specific concepts had been strongly debated: the definition of sugar and the problem of citrus concentrates. Senator John Breaux, our good friend but not totally on our side because of these issues, had suggested that a letter be written to clarify the concept of sugar, which in effect was somewhat confusing if you tried to look at it that way. A U.S. sugar industry executive wrote a letter to Senator Breaux in effect taking NAFTA hostage:

The NAFTA is in serious trouble in Congress and does not need sugar industry opposition. If the sugar industry's concerns were adequately resolved that opposition would be withdrawn. Our last vote count showed at least eighteen House members currently undecided or opposed to the NAFTA that could vote for the agreement if sugar's concerns were adequately solved.

The problem became clearer by the day. In the NAFTA text, Mexico will be able to export sugar to the United States once it is proven that it is a net surplus producer. This was to impede Mexico in exporting its sugar to the United States while at the same time importing from other countries for local consumption. The U.S. concern was that Mexico could become a sugar cane surplus producer by using fructose made of corn to be a sweetener for soft drinks. The proposal, based on a certain ambiguity in the text, was to include a letter stating that the definition of sugar included fructose. Our great concerns were first of all to convince the Mexican sugar industry and citrus growers that this would not be too harmful to their interests, and to be sure that we would really get the whole group to declare for NAFTA. At various times we counted 16, 14, or 12 votes that could be swayed with those interpretations.

The modification in sugar was to interpret the term "sugar and syrup goods consumed" to include fructose (tariff item 1702.40), chemically pure fructose (tariff item 1702.50), and fructose and fructose syrup under tariff item 1702.60. Fructose is a sweetener made mostly of corn. The modification thus meant that Mexico could not import fructose as a substitute for cane sugar in soft drinks—fructose's primary use—thereby becoming soon a net exporter of sugar and being able to access freely the U.S. market. Fructose could certainly be produced in Mexico, but the investment would be very high, and what the country most needed was the development of its sugar cane industry because it employed thousands of people in the countryside—farmers on unirrigated lands who for survival needed labor opportunities provided by the sugar cane harvest during the winter months. Thus the final redefinition would be painful to Mexico but not grievous, because the conversion of soft-drink sweeteners to fructose would require heavy investments and take time. Besides, the taste of a sugar-cane-sweetened soft drink is certainly preferred by most Mexican consumers.

On the citrus side, what the United States wanted were safeguards beyond those already established in NAFTA. The concept was to have the tariffs for orange juice go back to former levels under certain conditions, snapping a price and a quantity trigger. The price trigger would start if the daily closing price for fresh concentrate orange juice would for five consecutive business days drop below the monthly average for the most recent 5-year average. The quantity trigger would start if imports from Mexico reached 40 million gallons during a calendar year. In our opinion that would not damage the Mexican industry too much in the following 10 years.

These eleventh-hour demands reflected the political clout of the groups involved far more than the importance of the issues to the United States as a whole. In fact, the sugar industry is one of the most protected, and the impact of Mexican sugar would be negligible. The same could be said about the citrus industry where competition did not arise from Mexico but from Brazil. U.S. imports from Mexico in fact amounted to 5 percent of all U.S. imports, and it would take a long time for Mexico to grow trees to cause any concern to U.S. interests. But these interests had to be accommodated, and our concern was whether the votes promised would in fact materialize. A similar case had been the NADBank, where after much negotiation we had gotten one vote, giving rise to the joke: "one bank, one vote."

Our team had undertaken a risk assessment relating to the amount of votes we would gain in different alternatives regarding these issues. We had estimated that 23 members of Congress with some sugar interests would most likely remain opposed even with a sugar reconsideration. In some cases sugar was a factor but for other reasons a member would be likely to support NAFTA. In a large number of cases, 37 representatives by our count, sugar was not a central issue, although the members had sugar-producing districts. Another group of 15 members could, we thought, be motivated into supporting NAFTA with pressure from NAFTA-winners in their districts. These were our targets. This analysis had been done some time before, but we had now to weigh very carefully the proposal supported by some friends and the USTR. If things were not complicated enough, the two issues of citrus and sugar intersected in several districts. Thus the granting of one concession may probably not be sufficient. It was anybody's guess what the outcome would be, but we could not leave things to chance. So we studied all possible combinations. Among the potential votes were some also affected by the treatment of peanuts, tomatoes, winter vegetables, and flat glass. Sugar and citrus issues were a joint consideration for 11 of the members who would supposedly join NAFTA supporters if the clarifications were made. A second tier of 5 members more could finally join them. If only the sugar issue were addressed, we would get most likely 7 votes with another 5 in a second tier. On the night of November 2, we got little sleep as we went over the names of the 19 first-tier members involved and discussed with our political consultants the likelihood of this happening. After much deliberation we came out with a new, slightly different count of 8 Democrats and 3 Republicans who would be swayed toward us if we agreed to this reinterpretation. At our count before the sugar-citrus deal was made and not including the members thus considered, the opponents had 198 votes and the pro-NAFTA forces only 177. With 15 coming our way as a likely last count and with them losing 7 they could have counted upon, the count was at a balanced 192 in our favor and 191 in the opponent camp. There was also a promise to sit down after NAFTA was already in force and consider the possibility of a more rapid transition period for certain goods imported into Mexico like glass, but no commitment was made as to the final result. Finally a deal was made, and we were from then on confident that we had broken through the sound-barrier into victory – but it was not yet in our hands.

The final vote gave us great confidence in our analysis. Of the 11 we thought we were highly confident about, we lost only one – Jack Fields, a Republican from Texas. Another 3 votes of the proposed group finally came to our side.

Vote Count

Other representatives and senators started declaring for NAFTA. Carol Moseley-Braun of Illinois, the first black senator in U.S. history, had impressed me personally with her intelligence and charm. She had strong ties with labor, and her decision was therefore momentous and symbolically important.

By late October almost all counts gave a lead to the NAFTA opponents. For instance, on its count for October 31 the Knight-Ridder newspapers survey reported a 165-for to 200-against margin. Still on November 15 the Associated Press reported 181 members for and 202 against. We had been following the trend very closely in our operations room at our office and had been alarmed by the mounting opposition during October through early November, but started seeing a drift toward us, as is clear from the following table.

Changes in Member Positions
(members added to different positions during given periods)

	Period			
Rating*	October 4–8	October 11–15	November 1–11	November 15–19
1	10	8	40	69
2	11	5	44	5
4	16	9	9	5
5	27	14	36	22

*Ratings indicate the following: 1–for NAFTA; 2–leaning toward; 3–undecided; 4–leaning against; 5–opposed to NAFTA.

The changes were not always unambiguous and firm. Positions among the wavering crowd fluctuated continuously like the political weather. We identified 135 members who during the period September 1 through November 16 had changed their positions more than once, and several were engaged in a real political ballet. Bill Orton of Utah changed in five recorded steps from an initial favoring to a final opposition. Harold Ford from Tennessee and Floyd Flake of New York went through three steps from opposing to favoring. Overall vote counts differed some, but our calculations denoted a trend, as the following table shows.

Vote Count

Date	Rating*				
	1	2	3	4	5
Oct. 30	101	50	82	70	131
Nov. 2	123	112		191	
Nov. 5	114	73	50	48	149
Nov. 14	160	43	30	23	179
Nov. 15	166	41	27	21	179
Nov. 16	200	16	21	14	183
Nov. 17 (actual vote)	234				200

Source: Nov. 2, rating by the Bureau of National Affairs; Nov. 5, by the White House; the remainder, our estimations.

*For meaning of ratings, see note on previous table.

As the final days were arriving, there were still boasts by David Bonior to the effect that they were 2 votes short of a majority. Later, on November 15, according to that day's *Congress Daily*, he was counting a firm 223 votes. Duncan Hunter, Republican from California and Gerald Solomon, Democrat from New York, stepped into an almost empty House to proclaim they had 225 votes. This was untrue as the final result showed. Nevertheless, according to WTO counts, they were at the time just 9 votes away from victory. What had happened? Was it a fake or a bad count or a betrayal of votes that had already been committed to them? Probably a bad and wishful count to begin with.

One of the highly important forces behind the pro-NAFTA group was the good understanding and sharing of information on the subject of Democrats and Republicans. On the Republican side, Dreier of California and Kolbe of Arizona were of paramount importance. Kolbe understands trade issues very well and is intellectually of high caliber. Dreier is a charming, indefatigable proponent with political acumen. Finally on the Republican side, Newt Gingrich, the newly elected leader of the minority upon the stepping down of Robert Michel, thrust his strong personality for the NAFTA. It was his first challenge after becoming an anointed heir of Republican leadership in the House, and he used it adroitly. The three of them had good relationships with the actual whip—although not the formal one—of the democratic vote, Bill Richardson. Bill is a natural tactician; he feels politics like a breeze. He has an inner sense of the forcefully possible—which means possible after a hard push.

Although in certain aspects he is very liberally oriented, he is not a zealot—or a fake-zealot as is, in my mind, Gephardt. He is a pragmatist as is Gingrich, and thus both collaborated on their mutual vote-count. They stood on firm ground. Bonior, on the other hand, is certainly a man of courage and of principle and not a liar. What happened was that his count went wrong. He did not have as good a relation with his Republican allies-in-opposition-to-NAFTA and relied too much on Rep. Duncan Hunter.

Two other Democrats were extremely important to the outcome. One of them was Robert Matsui from California, a smooth and strong Californian of Japanese origin. He had been handed the job of Democratic whip because he was a member of the Ways and Means Committee, which had the strongest claim to jurisdiction in this process. Richardson, who thought he deserved the job, was gracious and worked in his usual forceful manner with Matsui. The other force with the Democrats was Dan Rostenkoski who, in spite of his being at the time distracted by the post-office-stamp scandal that later did him in, saw the implementing legislation through his most important committee and was always a strong proponent as he had been at the start of the whole process during the fast-track vote.

On November 17, the final day arrived for the scheduled vote in the House. The rule was approved easily even by people who would be against. The strategy used on the floor for the vote was intelligent and efficiently carried out. There was a stampede of votes favoring NAFTA immediately after the vote started providing the impression—a real one in this case—that it would be approved by a good margin. There are always some members of Congress who wait until the last moment, hedging before they vote. If the favorable votes had initially simply trickled down, it would have given some the impression of disaster, and they might have changed their votes. This obviously works on both sides. Finally the deciding 218th vote was delivered, and victory was ours.

The Mexican Washington team members, with our chief negotiator Herminio Blanco, who had been with us during the last weeks, were watching the vote on TV, having declined an invitation to attend Congress at a special booth because we preferred the intimacy of holding together. Champagne bottles were opened upon hearing the decisive vote, and we felt that all our efforts had met with great success. The mood in the House was also one of nervous tension. A good friend of mine and a competent and energetic Washington insider, Dan Flanagan, wrote a note to me: "On the day preceding the vote on the NAFTA in the House of Representatives, I had been invited—along with my son Clay—to sit in the Speaker's Gallery for the occasion. We were very fortunate as the Capitol was very crowded; in fact, in all my years in Washington I had never seen such lines stretching through the hallways! There was electricity in the air—the atmosphere of the House was pulsating. History was being made. The two countries were finally admitting their friendship."

Mexicans have a decisive competitive—an economist would say comparative—advantage at improvising a fiesta. We rose to our reputation and had a wonderful party first in my personal office, where the ones who could fit in had watched TV, and later at "El Jaleo," Spanish restaurant where, among others, my son Alejandro, a student at Georgetown University, and my wife Ibone joined us, still exhilarated by the exciting vote. They had watched from the Gallery. They were not appreciative of the long waiting lines though, which I found tremendous. Before getting to the "Jaleo," I went with Dr. Blanco for an interview with Hispanic and Mexican television to the roof garden of a building with the magnificent scenery of Washington by night. The lighted Capitol and Washington monument provided a most appropriate backdrop. Just as we finished, upon getting into the elevator the cellular phone rang. Dr. Blanco answered it, stepped out of the elevator, and was obviously caught by the call. It was President Salinas congratulating him on his success. In the embarrassing seconds of listening to the president, Dr. Blanco uttered the words: "Yes, Mr. President, it came about as we had forecast in our model" – referring to an econometric model that he and Luis de la Calle had estimated, based among other elements upon the outcome of the two fast-track votes that were mentioned earlier. The president spontaneously answered: "Herminio, one should trust more on people than on models. Congratulations to you and your team." It was a great remark that filled our hearts with joy.

President Clinton had had an active role at the end, but his whole administration's relation to the NAFTA issue was full of ambiguities with bursts of decisive action followed by internal confusion. The question is: how much did President Clinton actually contribute to the passage of NAFTA with his intermittent lack of focus? During the fast-track vote, Republican Bush got 95 Democratic votes. For NAFTA itself, Clinton got 100 Democratic votes. This does not necessarily mean that his influence was marginal. The opposition to NAFTA was much more belligerent than it had been on the fast-track approval, and one has to count many more votes to the credit of the president, although one has to grant him that NAFTA – thanks to him and President Bush as well – had become a highly contentious issue.

The greatest hurdle had been passed, but final victory still lay ahead. The Senate had yet to vote, although everybody had assured us that the Senate presented no great problems. But problems began of a different, almost innocent sort for people savvy in the ways of Congress. The House Rules Committee precisely defines the rules that will be followed in an upcoming floor debate, and the House as a whole ratifies the rule before the debate begins. No such mechanism exists in the Senate, however. The reason harks back to efforts of smaller states to resist being overwhelmed by the political power, represented in the number of congressional members, of the larger states. Thus more leeway has been traditionally granted to the way business is conducted in the Senate.

In the case of the NAFTA vote, a tactically relevant element existed: the Senate would adjourn after the NAFTA vote. The Senate majority leader controls the clock, restricted only by an existing cap, if any. The leader can elect to interrupt the clock to accomplish other legislative ends. In this case, the Senate debate that began on November 19 was interrupted by passage of a conference report on an unemployment insurance extension and the Brady bill on gun control. The leadership used NAFTA as leverage to keep the senators in Washington and have them vote on the rest of the agenda. In other words, they took NAFTA hostage to pass the other bills without any other mischievous idea. As a very fine consultant of ours, Howard Liebengood, once told me: "There are few things the Senate does with less grace than adjourn." NAFTA was of interest to all senators, the ones favoring and the ones opposing, and they were determined to stay. But the long debate—20 hours permitted—was interrupted by consideration of the other points. On Friday, we, the Mexican team, were anxiously waiting for a vote. We became rather nervous when the debate continued into Saturday with consideration of the other points as if NAFTA did not matter. We were particularly bewildered by Senator Gramm, whom we knew to favor NAFTA but who was apparently blocking the vote by talking against unemployment insurance. The tactics were not pretty but probably very effective. The leadership knew they had the vote on NAFTA—so had we been told—and its importance enabled them to play the leverage game to pass the other agreements.

Scholastics in the Middle Ages, it is said, spent their time considering how many times an angel's hair could be sliced. For me, a simple Mexican turned out to witness the actual workings of the U.S. political system, it seemed that Congress, in its sovereign ability to define its and the nation's rules, were engaged in a similar mind-boggling process. "*E puor si muove,*" as Galileo said—and yet it moves. After everything was said and done, the Senate moved, and by a substantial majority NAFTA—through its implementing legislation—became the law of the land.

Epilogue

At dawn on January 1, 1994, the day NAFTA began, a group of guerrilla fighters took over the town of San Cristobal in the mountainous and green Mexican state of Chiapas with the battle cry: Stop NAFTA! And yet we had talked about the overwhelming support of the people for the trade agreement.

During NAFTA's first year, political assassinations shocked the country. On March 23, 1994, the presidential candidate of the government party, the PRI, was shot down by a lone gunman, according to the official version; the people, however, almost unanimously believed it to be the work of a conspiracy—one probably led by politicians. In August 1994 in Mexico City, the secretary general of the PRI was shot down after a political breakfast in front of hundreds of onlookers. Many people were kidnapped, and bank robberies were rampant. And yet we had said that NAFTA would help lock in the reforms the country had undertaken, and Robert Zoellik, undersecretary of state, had said, in the U.S. Senate's first hearing, that it would help have a more stable neighbor to the South.

During 1994 the country was caught in political turbulence unknown in the previous 60 years. And yet President Salinas had said Mexico would not repeat Russia's experience of the Gorbachev era, when political reform had preceded economic restructuring, resulting in a fragile political system and a collapsed economy.

In the last month of 1994, Mexico suffered a traumatic devaluation that precipitated an international financial crisis. The predictions of our most vocal and virulent opponents about the pending devaluation of the peso once the agreement was signed were shown – although with some delay – to be a better forecast than our assertions of economic stability in the future.

Probably the most important point in the Salinas agenda had been the trade agreement with the United States; it had great symbolic value because it brought together many of the reforms he had undertaken. Mexico had been ushered into the club of developed countries at the Rue de la Muette in Paris, the head-quarters of the OECD. Yet scarcely two months after Salinas left office, the U.S. Congress was about to reject a multi-billion-dollar aid package in the midst of a crisis that apparently dashed any aspirations Mexico may have had to be counted in the foreseeable future among the developed countries of the world.

A black and uncouth Mexico had risen to give the lie to our message about the profound changes the country had undertaken toward becoming a "new" Mexico. Apparently we had been deluded and had in the process deceived others. Or, as our Mexican opponents always argued, Mexico was not ready for an agreement that meant giving away much of its industry and sovereignty, and the first encounter with its formidable neighbor had rent the whole fabric of the country.

Despite the reality of these problems, they had little to do with NAFTA itself but certainly much to do with the uneven transformation of a whole country – of which NAFTA provides a basic element. The insurgence in Chiapas – although it occurred under the anti-NAFTA banner – had been organized years before the NAFTA negotiations ever began by its leader, a Mexican activist intellectual who had experience in Sandinista Nicaragua and went by the name Sub-comandante Marcos. The group called itself the EZLN (Ejército Zapatista de Liberación Nacional or Zapata Army for National Liberation) after the peasant leader Zapata, who during the 1910s fought for land for the impoverished peasants. The group's profound grievance – the exploitation of indigenous peoples—is centuries old and has certainly proven that the transformation of the country has tremendous shortcomings. But it is unrelated to NAFTA except in its propaganda value, which its leaders have promoted with spectacular success.

In one aspect, however, the insurgence may have been NAFTA-conditioned. Probably the Salinas administration was aware that armed groups were being organized in the jungle and the beautiful cool forests of Chiapas, because of articles published in the newspapers. Also, *Proceso*, a weekly magazine critical of the government, had carried a story about a Jesuit missionary, coincidentally a childhood classmate of mine, who had provided evidence about them. But the government chose not to act, probably hoping to skirt a problem that would have made the ratification of NAFTA in November nearly impossible. In that purely expedient sense there was probably a link. The administration could have acted immediately afterward but wanted to avoid tainting its newly acquired international recognition. Most probably it really never fathomed the importance of the insurgence and was totally unprepared because, as events would show, it was taken by surprise on the very day it happened.

The turmoil in the political system that caused assassinations and so much upheaval around the presidential elections of August 1994 were not related to NAFTA. Neither was civil unrest causing so much violence and insecurity, although they were the effects of an overall transformation of which NAFTA was a positive, constructive element.

The Mexican political system in the twentieth century developed out of the convulsions of a bloody civil war that ravaged the country until the mid-1920s. At that time, the lack of political integration meant that warlords controlled different parts of the country, fighting each other and conspiring against each other to grasp the presidency. President Calles, himself a product of those intermittent wars, had a brilliant idea and enough clout to implement it. He assembled all those chieftains into a single political party in whose bosom the principles that led the civil war would blossom. This became the PRI, the governing party from 1927 to the present. It gave the political system a stability the country lacked, permitted different groups to operate within it, maintained strict discipline once a decision had been taken, and permitted a "circulation of the elites" with new groups being formed within its structure. But this structure was authoritarian in character and tended to stifle democratic opposition outside its ranks—and sometimes within them. It neglected the rise of corruption among its members because, as Lord Acton said, "Absolute power corrupts absolutely."

By controlling the most important levers of power, the system achieved an extraordinary cohesion and hold over the social and economic fabric of society. The private sector was highly protected from outside competition, and the government could directly intervene in almost all economic sectors because it directly owned and managed firms across the whole spectrum of the economy—from banks, steel mills, and textile factories to restaurants to the energy and petrochemical sectors. Any protest would have to be subdued lest the administration make use of its great powers to restrain criticism. The private and the communal (*ejïdo*) properties of the agricultural sector provide an example. A government entity, Conasupo, established prices for the most important crops, financed the harvest, and bought the produce. The ejido farmer was more subject to political influence, however, because almost all his financing and crop insurance came from the government; he could also be deprived of the land he harvested because in principle it was not his. The trade union leaders, as official members of the PRI, were part of the political system and held many positions as governors, senators, or members of congress. It does not mean they did not defend workers' rights, but only within certain limits. Finally, another element in Mexican society, also highly important, had few legal rights and could therefore voice few concerns related to social and political matters—the Church. Its priests could not vote, and because the Roman Catholic Church (or any other church) could own no properties, its buildings belonged to the state.

The government's grip over all of society and its ability to tighten it whenever necessary produced an atmosphere detrimental to the development of a grass-roots democratic system. Elections were certainly held, and probably most of them were in fact won by government party candidates. But the sheer weight of the government and its party were so strong that they could easily stifle, or delay, the growth of significant opposition. Democracy is not decreed by law—such laws had existed in Mexico for more than a century. It needs certain personal and corporate attitudes and a particular kind of culture to prosper.

Over the decades of the "pax PRI-ana" stability, Mexico made great strides and developed a young middle class—probably "lower" middle class by U.S. economic standards—that was educated and had, and has, a different social and political attitude. Here lay the seeds of a great transformation that was pushed—with inconsistencies certainly—by the administrations of both Presidents Miguel de la Madrid and Carlos Salinas. Salinas took over the momentum of the previous administration and boldly achieved enormous, if uneven, success in modernizing the country. The government gave up, one by one, many of the instruments it used to impose its will on society. It ceased most of its direct intervention in the economy, opened the border to foreign competition, dismantled the Conasupo as a forceful agent, provided for a change of communal to private property if the beneficiaries so determined, and recognized the legal status of the Catholic Church—and all other churches, although they do not have the same social significance in Mexico. The past two administrations have thus established conditions for Mexico to develop an authentic democracy and become a modern society.

The disturbances and instability that have plagued the country since 1994 are only the irremediable cost of changing from a stable but authoritarian and centralized system to a more open one. Forces have been unleashed that push—sometimes with strident, less than civilized manners—for a new configuration. Old power-brokers resist change and occasionally have few scruples as to how to avoid them. In a country whose native populations had been conquered and not always fully integrated into the social fabric, rapid transformation has revealed the anachronism and inhumanity of the old system. Ageless grievances have burst forth. This is the price that a society undergoing a profound, if peaceful, revolution has to pay. The July 1997 elections for the Mexican Congress and a number of governorships (including the governor of Mexico City, a newly created post) were the fairest in

Mexican history and were accepted as such by the political parties. These elections mark the end of the old system and provide a solid base for the continuing peaceful transformation of society.

Some ironies and inconsistencies in the policies applied toward transformation have mocked the vision. President Salinas sought first to implement economic reform, and although he established the possibility of democratic transformation, he was probably not altogether prepared for its speed. He led those reforms in an authoritarian manner that conflicted with the intended result and fueled the violent criticism of his tenure. But probably the hysterical, virulent condemnation of him personally had to do more with frustrated expectations than with anything else.

The role of NAFTA in this whole process is paramount. Many elements of Mexico's ongoing transformation are crystallized in the agreement, which gives them international stature. In my opinion, its most important aspect, reaching far beyond the tariff reductions and the investment flows that it will foster, is the transparency that NAFTA entails. New regulations pertaining to things that may affect commerce—and most of them do—need to receive public notice and be publicly discussed. This crucial element of democracy is a far cry from Mexico's old authoritarian mores. NAFTA is not only an economic document for Mexico but one with important consequences for the running of its political and social systems as well.

On December 1, 1994, a new president, Ernesto Zedillo, was sworn in. His cabinet comprised several people who had been directly involved in the NAFTA negotiations. On December 19, 1994, the financial system of Mexico collapsed. The peso was devalued as Ross Perot, among others, had predicted. The connection with NAFTA was, for many people, obvious. Either the Mexican government had belatedly done what Mr. Perot said—and that would shrink many of the exporting benefits that the United States would reap—or Mexico had been found unequal to the challenge set by U.S. competition. U.S. opponents tended to stress the first; Mexican opponents raised the second forcefully.

But as a matter of objective fact, NAFTA is wholly unrelated to what happened. For too long, Mexico had retained an overvalued currency that fostered a current account deficit in the balance of payments. This deficit was increasingly financed by short-term capital inflows, and for 1995 the country faced the repayment of close to $40 billion of debt in a situation where political instability and increased U.S. interest rates, among other factors, reduced these inflows. Further, the very instability that had ravaged the Mexican political system had raised doubts among investors and had led to outflows of capital and the dwindling of reserves. None of this was due to the effects of NAFTA. Some people and institutions, like the Bank of Mexico in its annual report, tend to underline the political factors as determining the lack of international confidence. Others insist upon the overvaluation of the peso and its sequel. Yet either arrogance of power, the overconfidence of an accumulated success record, or a simple lack of adequate analysis—or probably all of the above—led the Salinas government to persist in its misplaced short-term economic policies.

NAFTA's record is blameless with regard to the crisis and quite successful in spite of mounting adverse political and economic conditions. Mexico enjoys increasing trade with the United States and Canada, and its then moderate commercial deficit with those countries was certainly not the cause of the crash. NAFTA has lived up to its promises and has enormous potential to strengthen the long-term development of the country as well as reinforce its commercial ties with its partners.

Indirectly, however, NAFTA may be somewhat related to the financial crisis. The reason for Mexico's failure to take timely preventive measures toward devaluation may have been to avoid giving credence to U.S. opponents. Also, the government, basking in its international success with NAFTA, may have assumed that Mexico had become inured to the vagrancies of capital movements affecting emerging markets. But this is as far as the connection goes.

The devaluation turned into near collapse because of the fragility of certain elements in the economic system. The banks has just undergone privatization and modernization, and manufacturing firms, still in the process of getting ready to compete, were flexing their muscles. The large devaluation with its corrective measures and the ensuing instability within the financial system delivered a hard blow. The condition of the manufacturing sector is more directly related to NAFTA. The banking system had been privatized in the years 1991–1993. Owned by the government in the previous decade, it was mostly a tool to finance budget deficits and had to start all over in the learning curve. It overreached, failed to be conservative enough, and ended up in late 1994 with large nonperforming portfolios. On the other side, many industrialists eager to compete with foreign firms entering the country and looking at open foreign markets started investing, renewing plant and equipment, and in the process increasing their liabilities. This was mostly a NAFTA-conditioned effect. The putting together of a large devaluation, of weak banks, and of manufacturing firms indebted in order to modernize risked generating an imploding effect and has made the domestic financial crisis extremely serious. But NAFTA is at most indirectly to blame. The main effect of the whole trauma that the country is undergoing will be to correct that greatest of economic distortions—an overvalued peso. Once the spasmodic reactions of the financial system ended, the harsh medicine administered to the country by the Zedillo administration had set it back on a path toward stable growth. The country will continue to improve as it builds on the solid foundations established in the past.

NAFTA has apparently been a failure in other, more convoluted ways. The introduction to this volume refers to NAFTA as a rediscovery of common interests and shared values. Yet 1997 found the United States and Mexico further apart than at any time since the U.S. Marines landed in Veracruz in 1914. Several factors were at work. Many people in the United States have felt deceived because they were hoping to bolster their southern neighbor toward its development as a young, dynamic, modern country, and the immediate outcome had been a financial crisis and the display of sordid stories of corruption, some related to drug trafficking. Yet, once again, this is unrelated to NAFTA. The difficult and complex task of modernizing a country has brought to the surface a great deal of corruption that previously lay under the heavy hand of the authoritarian regime.

As a society becomes more open, its underlying and hitherto

concealed problems are brought to light—a highly positive development because it means its political system is becoming more democratic and accountable. Clouding and complicating the process is the tendency of some U.S. politicians to grab the opportunity to blame foreigners for problems that are largely domestic. All demand, if money-backed, creates its own supply. Demand for illegal drugs creates illegal supply because of the huge profits involved. One has to fight for cooperation on both sides, but it is always easier to blame the neighbor.

Further, the discovery of old ingrained corruption provides an irresistible target for the hypocritical wrath and revenge of groups who from the beginning were opposed to NAFTA. But the spirit of NAFTA will prevail as Mexico sheds its authoritarian past and as the United States increases its understanding of the difficult yet hopeful process that is leading the two countries toward a better future of friendly partnership. President Clinton's strong, quick reaction to the financial crisis in early 1995 and Mexico's recovery and prompt repayment of the funds received are a harbinger of better things to come.

Another intriguing connection between NAFTA and the Mexican devaluation crisis and financial collapse provided scurrilous arguments against the agreement. It is of a personal nature. The new administration of President Zedillo, which took office on December 1, 1994, was heavily staffed by former members of the NAFTA team. Secretary of Treasury Jaime Serra had, as secretary of commerce at the time, been the chief official responsible for NAFTA. Secretary of Commerce Herminio Blanco had been my direct boss and chief negotiator of the agreement. Secretary of Labor Santiago Oñate had been the man responsible for the environmental negotiations during the side agreements. The position of comptroller—a cabinet post—was held by Norma Samaniego, who had been in charge of the labor team during the side agreements. The chief of staff to the president, Luis Téllez, had been in charge of agricultural problems in NAFTA. Secretary of Transportation Carlos Ruíz Sacristán had participated in a senior position in the financial services chapter. It was and is notoriously a NAFTA cabinet. Although common experience in NAFTA has given it coherence and depth of understanding, any errors tend to boomerang and be considered NAFTA errors. The same should be said about success, which has been far more prevalent on both the economic and political scenes.

One person had to make the dramatically difficult decision to devalue, and, according to popular sentiment, his handling of it made him highly responsible for the outcome. He was none other than Dr. Jaime Serra, the shortest-lived finance minister in Mexican history, having resigned less than a month after the inauguration. He will have to tell the story of his own involvement, but he had been given a bad hand to play – and he played it hesitantly.

Dr. Blanco received, owing to his success in NAFTA and his undeniable talents, the most unenviable task of becoming the secretary of commerce at a time of unexpected explosive inflation. Inflation was not caused by acts of that department, but in Mexican tradition the public blames Commerce for price rises. At one time, before the modernization, it mandated the prices of many of the goods sold. Blanco has to try to control the effects of other ministries' policies, and, if that were not enough, is also responsible for industrial promotion. Great criticism is being raised about the lack of an industrial policy to help the manufacturing sector get on its feet at a time of company failures. As a reward for his fantastic contribution to NAFTA, he received a wild tiger and the most unwelcome task of taming him.

Finally, former president Salinas, who had first uttered the idea of engaging in a Free Trade Agreement with the United States in Davos and courageously held the rudder tight on occasions when political conditions in the United States jeopardized the negotiations, is living in self-imposed exile as the person the majority of Mexicans blame as the worst president in recent decades. Fickle and vain is the world, and frail is human fame.

As "dramatis personae" who had a splendid performance on the NAFTA stage, all three of the Mexican officials most responsible for NAFTA – Salinas, Serra, and Blanco – have had truly dramatic roles to play in the aftermath of their, and their country's, great success.

Appendix
Key Points in the NAFTA Negotiations

June 10, 1990

President Bush and President Salinas issue a joint statement endorsing the idea a comprehensive free trade agreement between the United States and Mexico and direct their trade ministers to undertake consultations and preparatory work.

August 8, 1990

U.S. Trade Representative Carla A. Hills and Mexican secretary of commerce Jaime Serra-Puche report back to the two presidents, jointly recommending the initiation of formal negotiations.

August 21, 1990

President Salinas writes to President Bush proposing that the United States and Mexico negotiate a free trade agreement, a step required by U.S. law.

September 25, 1990

President Bush writes to the chairmen of the House Ways and Means and Senate Finance committees notifying them, as required by U.S. law, of free trade negotiations with Mexico. In his letter, the president also informs the chairmen that Canada has expressed a desire to participate in the negotiations.

155

February 5, 1991

President Bush, President Salinas, and Canadian prime minister Brian Mulroney announce their intention to pursue a North American Free Trade Agreement, creating one of the world's largest liberalized markets.

February 5, 1991

President Bush writes to the chairmen of the House Ways and Means and Senate Finance committees of his desire to enter into trilateral negotiations with Mexico and Canada for a North American Free Trade Agreement (NAFTA).

February 6 & 20, 1991

Senate Finance Committee holds public hearings on the proposed negotiations.

February 20–21, 1991

International Trade Subcommittee of the House Ways and Means Committee holds public hearings on the proposed negotiations.

February 27, 1991

Sixty-day legislative review period expires, during which time the Senate Finance Committee or House Ways and Means Committee could have voted to deny fast-track procedures to legislation implementing a free trade agreement with Mexico.

March 1, 1991

President Bush requests a two-year extension of fast-track procedures for legislation implementing trade agreements, a necessary step if the procedures are to be used for NAFTA.

May 1, 1991

In response to congressional concern expressed during the fast-track debate, President Bush in a letter to Congress commits as follows: to consult extensively during the course of the negotiations and conduct a broad public outreach effort, to work to ensure that any negative impact on em-

ployment as a result of NAFTA is mini-
mized and assist dislocated workers by
ensuring an adequately funded worker adjustment program, to gradually phase out
duties over time with long transition periods for sensitive sectors, to include an effective safeguard mechanism, to provide
for strict rules of origin, and to address environmental and labor standards as well as
workers' rights issues.

May 3, 1991   U.S. labor secretary Lynn Martin and
                     Mexican minister of labor and social wel-
                     fare Arsenio Farell Cubillas sign a Memo-
                     randum of Understanding to promote
                     higher living standards and a safe and
                     healthy workplace for workers in the two
                     countries.

May 23–24, 1991   Consistent with President Bush's request,
                     both houses of Congress vote to extend
                     fast-track authority for two years for
                     NAFTA and for other purposes.

June 12, 1991   NAFTA negotiations formally launched
                     in Toronto, Canada, with trilateral meet-
                     ing of trade ministers; 19 working groups
                     convene.

June 23–25, 1991   U.S. Department of Commerce and the
                     USTR lead delegation of 19 industry sector
                     and functional advisory committee advisers
                     to Mexico for intensive two-day round of
                     meetings with Mexican government nego-
                     tiators, the Mexican private sector, and
                     U.S. companies operating in Mexico.

July 8–9, 1991   Plenary session in Washington, D.C.,
                     chaired by chief negotiators of the three
                     countries.

August 1, 1991	Draft U.S.-Mexico Border Plan released for public comment.
August 6–7, 1991	Plenary session in Oaxtepec, Mexico, chaired by chief negotiators of the three countries.
August 18–20, 1991	Second Trilateral Ministerial Oversight meeting held in Seattle, Washington.
August 21–September 11, 1991	Trade Policy Staff Committee conducts public hearings held in San Diego, Houston, Atlanta, Washington, D.C., Cleveland, and Boston. Several hundred witnesses testify.
September 19, 1991	The United States, Canada, and Mexico exchange initial tariff staging proposals and non-tariff barrier request lists at a meeting of the Tariffs and Non-Tariff Barriers Negotiating Group in Dallas, Texas.
October 17, 1991	USTR and EPA submit draft review of U.S.-Mexico Environmental Issues for public comment.
October 25–28, 1991	Third Trilateral Ministerial Oversight meeting in Zacatecas, Mexico.
December 14, 1991	President Salinas and President Bush in meeting at Camp David agree on importance of NAFTA and need for broad, comprehensive agreement.
December 31, 1991	Negotiators complete composite bracketed texts.
January 6–10, 1992	Meetings at Georgetown University in Washington, D.C., to prepare composite texts.

January 16–17, 1992	Chief negotiators meet to review negotiations in Washington, D.C.
February 2–3, 1992	Ambassador Carla A. Hills leads delegation of 26 private sector representatives and 11 members of Congress to Mexico. Delegation meets with President Salinas, Secretary of Commerce Serra, and other key Mexican government and private sector officials.
February 9–10, 1992	Fourth Trilateral Ministerial Oversight meeting held in Chantilly, Virginia.
February 10–12, 1992	U.S. and Mexican officials, along with organized labor, hold hazardous industry conference focusing on iron and steel industry.
February 17–21, 1992	Plenary session in Dallas, Texas, chaired by chief negotiators of the three countries.
February 25, 1992	President Bush receives NAFTA Environmental Review and Environmental Border Plan from USTR Carla A. Hills and EPA administrator William K. Reilly in Los Angeles, California.
February 26, 1992	President Salinas and Minister Serra, in San Antonio, Texas, to attend Drug Summit, meet to discuss NAFTA progress with President Bush and Carla Hills.
March 4–5, 1992	Plenary session in Washington, D.C., chaired by chief negotiators of the three countries.
March 23–27, 1992	Plenary session in Washington, D.C., chaired by chief negotiators of the three countries.
April 6–8, 1992	Fifth Trilateral Ministerial Oversight meeting held in Montreal, Canada.

April 27–May 1, 1992	Plenary session in Mexico City, Mexico, chaired by chief negotiators of the three countries.
May 13–15, 1992	Plenary session in Toronto, Canada, chaired by chief negotiators of the three countries.
June 1–5, 1992	Plenary session in Crystal City, Virginia, chaired by chief negotiators of the three countries.
June 17–19, 1992	Chief negotiators meet to review negotiations in Washington, D.C.
June 29–July 3, 1992	Chief negotiators meet to review negotiations in Washington, D.C.
July 7–10, 1992	Chief negotiators meet to review negotiations in Washington, D.C.
July 14, 1992	Presidents Bush and Salinas and their trade ministers, Hills and Serra, meet to discuss status of the NAFTA talks and announce the beginning of the final stage of negotiations.
July 25–26, 1992	Sixth Trilateral Ministerial Oversight meeting held in Mexico City, Mexico.
July 29–August 12, 1992	Chief negotiators meet to review and finalize negotiations in Washington, D.C.
August 2–12, 1992	Seventh Trilateral Ministerial Oversight meeting to finalize NAFTA in Washington, D.C.
August 12, 1992	The two presidents and the prime minister of Canada announce the completion of negotiations for NAFTA. Several documents are issued, including a negotiated summary of the agreement.

August 13–September 16–18, 1992	Legal staff work on the draft agreement. In accordance with the 90-day notice requirement, President Bush officially notifies the Speaker of the House and the president of the Senate of his intent to enter into NAFTA. The notice is accompanied by reports of 38 private sector advisory committees on the draft agreement.
October 7, 1992	The two presidents and the prime minister meet in San Antonio, Texas, to discuss plans for implementing NAFTA. The three trade ministers who negotiated the agreement—Carla Hills, Jaime Serra, and Michael Wilson—initial the NAFTA draft legal test. Speaking in North Carolina, Democratic candidate Clinton comes out in support of NAFTA.
December 17, 1992	The two presidents and the prime minister sign NAFTA in their respective capitals. President-elect Clinton reaffirms his support of NAFTA, reiterating that three side agreements are required to cover environmental and labor problems and safeguards for any unexpected surge in imports.
January 1993	Clinton and Salinas meet in Austin.
January 1993	President Clinton is inaugurated as president.
January 1993	Mickey Kantor is confirmed as U.S. Trade Representative.
February 1993	Side agreement negotiation starts.

February 1993	Informal staff-level consultation between the USTR and committees of jurisdiction in the House and Senate start on required changes in the United States to implement NAFTA obligations.
March 8, 1993	The Speaker of the House reconvenes a Trade Agreement Coordinating Group chaired by the chairman of the Committee on Ways and Means. New prime minister takes office in Canada.
August 13, 1993	Trade ministers announce agreement by the three governments on labor and environmental cooperation and on import surges.
September 14, 1993	The NAFTA side agreements are signed in ceremonies at the three capitals.
September 28, 1993	In a letter to House Speaker Foley, President Clinton emphasizes the importance of Congress's voting on a bill to implement NAFTA before adjournment in 1993.
November 2, 1993	The Speaker of the House and the Senate majority leader transmit to the U.S. Trade Representative the proposed implementing legislation for NAFTA and proposals for inclusion in the Statement of Administrative Action.
November 4, 1993	President Clinton sends two letters of transmittal to the Congress conveying the NAFTA text, the implementing bill, the Statement of Administrative Action, the side agreements, and other documents. The side agreements do not require congressional approval but are part of the entire NAFTA package to be considered by Congress in deciding approval of the implementing bill.

Resolution H.R. 3450, introduced by Rep. Rostenkowski as designee of the majority leader and Rep. Archer as designee of the minority leader, proposes eight committees of jurisdiction.

Senate bill S. 1627 is introduced and referred only to the Committee on Finance.

November 15, 1993   House Ways and Means recommends passage; House Banking, Finance, and Urban Affairs recommend against passage; House Energy and Commerce committees report no recommendation.

Senate Finance Committee passes bill S. 1627.

November 17, 1993   House roll call approving NAFTA.

November 20, 1993   Senate roll call approving NAFTA.

January 1, 1994   NAFTA takes effect.

Index

About the Author

Hermann von Bertrab joined the Mexican government to assist in the NAFTA process, serving from December 1990 until May 1994 as head of the Washington office in charge of coordinating operations for public and governmental relations. Previously, he was involved in developing new businesses as founder and partner of Sinex, an exporter of processed commodities, and of Imerval, a financial training institute.

Dr. von Bertrab has held leading positions at various Mexican financial institutions. He was senior vice president in charge of investments at Bancomer and senior vice president for research and development at OBSA, an investment bank and brokerage firm now part of Grupo Serfin. He also headed the Business Development Division of Grupo Mexicano de Desarrollo.

Born in Tampico, Mexico, in November 1928, Dr. von Bertrab studied at the Iberoamericana University (Mexico) and at the University of Innsbruck (Austria). He pursued graduate studies in the United States at the Massachusetts Institute of Technology and received his Ph.D. in economics from the University of Texas (Austin). He has taught economics at the Monterrey Institute of Technology, the Universidad Iberoamericana, and the Universidad Lasalle.